QUILTS & COVERLETS

QUILTS & COVERLETS
A CONTEMPORARY APPROACH

JEAN RAY LAURY

PHOTOGRAPHS BY GAYLE SMALLEY

VAN NOSTRAND REINHOLD COMPANY
NEW YORK   CINCINNATI   TORONTO   LONDON   MELBOURNE

Frontispiece:
"Blue Garden" by the author; about 4' by 6'. Antique needlework combined with transparent fabrics are appliquéd to form flowers with net and organdy added for stems and leaves. The coverlet is not quilted.

Van Nostrand Reinhold Company Regional Offices:
New York   Cincinnati   Chicago   Millbrae   Dallas
Van Nostrand Reinhold Company International Offices:
London   Toronto   Melbourne

Drawings by the author
Photography by Gayle Smalley except where otherwise indicated
Designed by Rosa Delia Vasquez

Published by Van Nostrand Reinhold Company
450 West 33rd Street, New York, N.Y. 10001
Published simultaneously in Canada by
Van Nostrand Reinhold Ltd.

Foreword

It is indeed a paradox today that, as life moves toward standardization in many areas, it moves at the same time toward diversity of self-expression. This is true in the fine arts and in skills such as gourmet cooking, and it is true in needlework as well.

In over twenty years as a needlework editor, I have seen countless quilts and helped to judge many quilt exhibitions. It was at such an exhibition, about a decade ago, that I saw Jean Laury's first quilt—a delightful, completely unorthodox quilt depicting all the things that interested and excited her children, at that time very young. It was like a fresh breeze, the first contemporary quilt I had ever seen that really came off successfully; yet it was far simpler and more direct in stitchery than the many fine traditional quilts in the exhibition. It inspired me, soon afterward when I was making a trip to California, to seek out Mrs. Laury. Thus began what has been a long and fruitful friendship.

I am sure that Jean Laury has been an inspiration to others to take a new view of quilt making as a far more personal, yet also utilitarian, art relevant to our times. Quilting is an ancient technique, quite possibly first used to thicken wearing apparel for warmth and to pad armor for comfort in the Middle Ages. However, quilts as bedcovers, some purely utilitarian, others beautifully planned and embellished, have also been known for hundreds of years in Europe. So it was quite natural that quilts should play a part in America's beginnings and reflect the social changes that occurred as this country expanded. First fashioned out of the dire necessity to make use of every scrap of fabric, quilts later became a vehicle of keen competition at the country fairs and expositions that flourished in the nineteenth and even twentieth centuries.

Even while one marvels at the incredibly meticulous stitchery and variation of pattern of the early quilts, one must visualize the largely rural society of the times. Muddy roads caused isolation for weeks at a time, when neither wheel nor sleigh could travel. I have heard both quilts and hooked rugs referred to as "mud work," which indeed they were, with much of the time indoors being devoted to piecing or appliquéing the quilt top. When the weather broke, came, with a whoop and a holler, the great quilting party. The women quilted all day and the men arrived in the evening for the feasting and dancing. Everyone drove home tired, I'm sure, but happy, and probably many new romances were born.

Social conditions may once again affect quilt making as one of the greatest of American folk arts. We have become a mobile society and no longer have isolation to deal with. But we still have the need to preserve our own individuality by making things that delight the eye and convey the spirit of our times. I have always believed that use lends grace to anything we make; what better example is there than a quilt or a coverlet?

Roxa Wright
Needlework Editor
Woman's Day Magazine

Dedication

To the quilt makers of the past, of the present, and especially of the future.

Acknowledgments

My warmest thanks to Roxa Wright, needlework editor of Woman's Day Magazine, *and to Professor Matt Kahn of Stanford University, who both first encouraged my interest in quilts; to Frank B. Laury, for his perceptive assistance on this manuscript; to Gayle Smalley for the talent and time devoted to the photography; to Barbara Klinger for her helpful and able editing; and to all the quilt makers who so generously loaned their works to be used in the book.*

Contents

About Quilts

This book is for all who enjoy quilts or quilt making, and especially for those interested in the contemporary application of this traditional art form.

Anyone can make a quilt. The process may take time but it is not difficult. Whatever your sewing skills, drawing ability, or designing talents, they can be adapted to quilt making. In this book many ways of making quilts are described. Some are very simple and can be accomplished even by those with an absolute minimum of sewing ability or design experience. Others are more intricate and will inspire the person whose background in sewing or in art is extensive.

Women have always combined art with sewing in the tradition of quilt making. There are few of us who don't have a treasured old quilt from the past. We sometimes prize these antique quilts beyond reason, not understanding ourselves what it is that we most value in them. Each quilt brings us a glimpse of the person who made it, and provides a very personal link with the past. Through the colors selected, the chosen patterns and prints, the ideas used, and the care in the stitching, we know something of that person which is not communicated in any other way. We also sense the individual's values; for the workmanship and skill, as well as the artistry of the quilt, have made it an object that endures.

Quilts were made not only as utilitarian pieces but also because they offered women a medium of self-expression. The need for warmth led to the padding and layering of fabrics, just as the need to utilize fabric scraps led to piecing and patchwork. The necessity for durability produced careful and strong stitching. But it was the desire to add beauty to everyday articles of the home that led to the use of carefully arranged and selected mosaics of colored fabric. Beauty rather than economics accounted for the survival of quilts through so many years.

Time, use and wear enhance the surfaces of fabric as they do all other materials. Fabrics become soft, some colors fade, and there is a mellowing of the whole not unlike the patina on silver. This contributes to the pleasing appearance of old quilts.

"Blue Garden" (detail). The delicate patterns of the old-fashioned doilies are emphasized by the blue background. Leaves and stems are appliquéd with satin stitches and flowers are finished off with embroidery.

TROY IN THE TROJAN WAR
SIR TRISTRAM DEFEATED SIR MARHAUS FOR KING MARK OF CORNWALL
ROLAND FOUGHT THE MOORS FOR CHARLEMAGNE
WILLIAM THE CONQUEROR DEFEATED HAROLD AT THE BATTLE OF HASTINGS

"Heroes" by the author; four panels, each 2' by 9'. Each panel of this coverlet has a figure of appliquéd cotton commemorating a legendary hero. The panels were joined to each other and to a backing.

"Heroes" (detail). Satin stitches sewn by machine hold the appliquéd shapes to the fabric top and are also used for the lettering. Hand embroidery is used for the details in the figures.

The designs themselves also retain their appeal, though in quilt design —as in all crafts—styles and fashions change. At the time the quilt is produced the design may be seen as "up-to-date" or as "old-fashioned." It may be considered "stylish" or "dated." But this evaluation is determined by standards in vogue at that time and is always subject to change. Years later we can view the piece for what it is without being so affected by the arbitrary imposition of style. As styles change, we often find a new acceptance for the old. The "optical" and "pop" art forms of today are often found in early American quilts and are being newly appreciated. The former use of combinations of many different prints into dazzlingly complex quilt tops is now being adopted in contemporary fabrics and fashions. Piecing, appliqué, and quilting are all finding their way in today's clothing styles.

Our enjoyment of those quilts which have been passed along to us can stimulate the desire to make our own quilts, to contribute our own ideas in a quilt to be passed on to others. Quilts provide a lovely, fragile and personal kind of silent, visual communication from one generation to others.

"Tom's Quilt" (detail) by the author. Objects of interest to a child are formed from fabric shapes and appliquéd to blocks of fabric. The blocks are of varying shapes and are pieced together. The pieced top, a filler and a backing are held together with the quilting stitches within each block.

In looking at the old quilts we can sense what was important to that quilt maker—the wild flowers, the house depicted in this block, the figures of children, the puzzlelike arrangements of riotous colors. Making our own quilts provides us with an opportunity to define some of those things that are so important to us.

Quilt making offers enjoyment in the process itself as well as pleasure in the finished product. At its best, a quilt is a personal expression—not a mimic of the ideas or designs or color preferences set down by someone else. Original design is not beyond the capacity of any homemaker or student or quilt maker. If you have made quilts before, you will know which of the approaches offered here can be easily followed. If you are new to the world of quilt making, follow the suggestions indicating the quilts that are more suitable for beginners. If you have a background in art or design, you will find a whole new range of possibilities for your talents in working with the colors, patterns, compositions and textures of quilts.

There are many excellent books available on traditional quilts, and most of these contain photographs of some of the incredibly beautiful and de-

"Coat of Arms Quilt" by Jean Rafferty McLean; 32" by 42". The heraldic details of the shield are hand-appliquéd to the quilt top. The quilting stitches, sewn by machine, are closely related to the appliqué design and give it a sculptural quality.

tailed quilts of early America. However, very little attention has been given to the recent work that has grown out of this rich heritage. It is the dual purpose of this book to recognize the work of contemporary quilt makers and to encourage others to enjoy an art that unifies the practical and the aesthetic, the traditional and contemporary, and combines the structural solutions with interests in embellishment.

Presented in the following pages are two basic approaches to making quilts and coverlets. One approach is to begin with a large quilt-sized piece of fabric and to then add some embellishment to this surface by any of various means. The other is to take many small pieces of fabric, join them together in some predetermined way, and produce a single, large piece of fabric which becomes the quilt top.

The first category of quilts and coverlets uses what may be called an "applied top." That is, a decorative treatment is applied to the large, fabric top. The second category uses what is referred to as a "pieced top," one that is constructed of many small pieces. The book is divided into these two categories of quilt or coverlet tops based on the difference in structure.

"Coat of Arms Quilt," reverse side. Both the appliqué design and the elaborate quilting pattern are carried through to the back of the quilt by the machine-stitching. Quilt is filled with Dacron batting.

"Peace Quilt" by the author; each appliquéd block is 6½" by 7". Fabric squares with appliqué designs are joined to strips of cloth to form the quilt top. The blocks are emphasized by quilting stitches that go through the top fabric, the filler, and the backing.

"Peace Quilt," reverse side. The quilting stitches produce a raised pattern of block forms on the back of the quilt, which is one large piece of fabric.

Within each of these two approaches there are many variations, which are also shown. A third section of the book is devoted to the techniques of the actual quilting process, which is common to all quilts.

A quilt consists of three parts: the fabric top, decorated by an applied design or by the pattern of piecing; a second piece of fabric which provides the backing; and a third layer of filler or padding between. All three layers are then held together by quilting stitches.

Coverlets are usually lighter in weight than quilts and have little or no inner padding. They may consist of the top only, or they may be lined. If lined, the two layers may be "tied" together. Sometimes a quilting stitch is used, but it is rarely a dominant part of the design. Coverlets are not made for warmth, but rather are thought of as a decorative cover. Some quilt makers define coverlets only as being smaller in size, covering just the top of a bed. Other quilters use the words "coverlets" and "quilts" interchangeably. In this book, "quilts" will be used as the general term, and "coverlets" will be used to identify those lightweight covers in which the quilting is minimal.

In making a quilt today, you will be aware of certain changes from traditional modes of working and designing. Originally quilts were a means of utilizing precious bits and scraps of fabric. Though it served more than utilitarian functions—by bringing color, pattern and beauty into the home— quilt making was essentially a "salvage art." Many early quilt makers were artists. Others could manage the incredible workmanship required in the production of a quilt, but used designs devised by others. Nonetheless, all saved the scraps and remnants so essential for quilts, and each quilt was to some extent the result of the quilt maker's inventiveness within the limited range of her materials.

Today fabric shops dazzle us with an array of seemingly unlimited quantities of materials and colors, and we no longer feel the same need to salvage the unworn portions from old clothes. Our quilts can now be designed differently, recognizing the range of the materials available. We do not work under the same limitations.

The development of technology, which yielded this luxuriant supply of materials at reasonable prices, also gave us a sewing machine that can be utilized as an extension of the hand. It is possible to exert better control over these new machines than over previous ones. This makes the machine very sensitive to the influence of the designer, and the sewing machine generously adds to the possibilities from which the quilt maker can choose. The use of this efficient and versatile machine should not be regarded as an "impure" approach to quilting, but as a means of expanding the potentials of designing.

Today, our reasons for making quilts are clearly other than practical ones. One motivation is the need to personalize and individualize the articles of daily use. So many of the manufactured items we use repeatedly are identical to thousands of others. They are impersonal, anonymous, and without variation. Because of this, we especially enjoy and appreciate articles which are handmade. A quilt offers the opportunity to produce an article of personal value, both practical in nature and aesthetic in design.

Aesthetically, there is a directness of approach and an honesty of intent in a quilt that is easily comprehended by everyone. Quilt making is one of our few remaining folk arts. One of the distinguishing factors of any folk art is that the art objects are consumed, or used, by the people who produce them. Certainly this is true of quilts, as they are almost always made to be used in one's own home or in the home of a friend or a family member. Quilts are time-consuming and quilt makers usually become very personally involved in the designing. For this reason, a quilt maker is not likely to make quilts on a commercial basis. The hours and hours poured into a quilt, pleasantly spent as they are, can rarely be compensated for with money. It is a work of love, and a quilt is often something you would give away, but would not sell.

The aesthetic development of the quilt was directly affected by the Industrial Revolution, which put the handcrafts in a secondary position. The homemaker seemed totally infatuated with the glamour of machine-produced products. The power machine overshadowed handwork. Folded at the foot of the bed was the Sears and Roebuck Indian blanket, and the quilts were relegated to the role of padding old furniture stored in the attic or barn. Individual design was forgotten.

"The Seven Point Star," a pre-Civil War quilt, from the collection of Dorothy Bahrs Jacobus. Each star is pieced from many diamond-shaped cutouts of dark and light fabric, and each is appliquéd to a separate fabric block. This traditional quilt is entirely hand-sewn. (Photo by Barbara Klinger.)

The lack of vitality and relevance which characterized quilt design for many years led to an increased attention to the workmanship. Quilters vied to make quilts with more stitches than anyone else. If one person boasted a quilt containing so many thousands of stitches, another would announce a quilt which topped that record by hundreds or thousands more. The stitching no longer became a means by which the quilt was made; rather, it encompassed the whole purpose of quilt making. The stitches became the goal rather than the method of enhancement.

In addition, for many years, quilt making was unaffected by contemporary art. In early America, the sources for quilt designs came from nature and from all the articles of everyday use—the patterns on dishes, the designs from cast-iron stoves, political symbols such as the eagle and the star, wild flowers and other natural forms. In the twentieth century, however, none of the new influences of the time seem to have permeated quilt design. Even the strong influence of Art Nouveau, which was apparent in other crafts, had almost no effect on quilt making.

Perhaps women lost confidence in their ability to design. We saw watered-down versions of old designs, used over and over, with few of the revitalizing changes essential in any "lively" art. Only recently is the influence of contemporary art once again seen in our quilts. Modern designers of quilts are not concerned with reiterating statements made years ago. They have their own comments to make, comments which are relevant to our own times. Perhaps it is because, now that our homes are saturated with machined products, we can again begin to appreciate the special value of handcrafted articles, a value which comes from personal involvement.

Quilt makers today are recapturing the spirit and essence of early American quilts. At last we can look forward to exciting designs. Gone, thank goodness, are the rows upon rows of obese, sunbonnet girls in pale green and lavender. Traditional designs no longer meet our needs. Creativity and inventiveness make it possible to modify and rejuvenate the old approaches and techniques. Systems of construction in quilt making are strong, durable and beautiful. If we can retain the structural integrity of the traditional quilt, and add to it a contemporary approach in color and design, we will achieve a quilt which merges past and present.

Students, designers, and homemakers often ask where they will ever find the time to make a quilt. And it would be a rare occurrence when any one of them suddenly found herself graced with the two or three "free" months that might be required. It isn't necessary to have enough time to complete a quilt all at once. You only need time to make one quilt block. Then you find time to do a second block, and a third. Every hill is climbed step by step. In the same way, your quilt grows as you visit, while your cookies bake, when you wait at the dentist's office, ride in a car, or watch a television program. Taken one step at a time, the blocks accumulate. As your enthusiasm grows, you manage to find more time for your sewing. Your skills will also improve, and after doing just ten blocks you will find that your speed and incentive have greatly increased. Your problem will not be finding time to sew quilts, but rather finding time to do the shopping or cooking necessary to the running of a household.

A quilt is a wonderful, exciting, personal project and one which can involve an individual to whatever lengths she is willing and able to go. It is my hope that I can encourage others to find the satisfaction and enjoyment that awaits them in this venture.

Part I

APPLIED TOPS

Applied tops are those in which you start out with a full-sized fabric base to which you add the design elements. The structural unit for this kind of quilt or coverlet is already complete, and the basic top can be thought of as a large sheet of paper or a canvas on which to execute the design. The top is worked on all at once, not in sections. It is essential to determine the finished size of the quilt, cut the fabric, and—if necessary—piece yardage to the required dimensions before proceeding with the applied decorative work.

On this background material, you can then do a drawing, using threads and yarns; a painting, using batik or other dye-design processes; or a collage, using cut pieces of fabric. In using a linear approach, embroidery may be done either by hand or by sewing machine. In using a painterly approach, dyes may be applied directly to fabric. Without dyes, large pieces of fabric may be appliquéd to the base material, either completely covering the latter or incorporating it in the design. The application of many small pieces of fabric—such as printed labels or a series of appliqué-decorated blocks—creates the effect of a collage. Different treatments may be combined in making the applied top.

Plate 1. "Garden" by the author; 48" by 72". Hand-embroidered linear design creates overall motif on this crib-sized coverlet of white nylon. French knots are used to "tie" the quilt top, the flannel filler, and the backing together.

1. Single-Motif Design

One of the simplest ways to make a quilt top is to start with a single piece of fabric large enough to cover a bed and to then decorate the fabric with a single motif or central design. You may find it helpful to place the material over the bed to see it in position. Then you can begin to visualize the colors and forms which might be put on the surface of that cover.

If the materials for your quilt top must be pieced in order to have a fabric large enough to cover the bed, then the seams themselves might become a part of the design. For example, on a single bed, fabric which is one yard wide would cover the top, and the sides could be added. That puts the seam in a logical position regarding the shape of the bed. This would also provide a good space division if the side panels were to be of another color. (See Figure 1.)

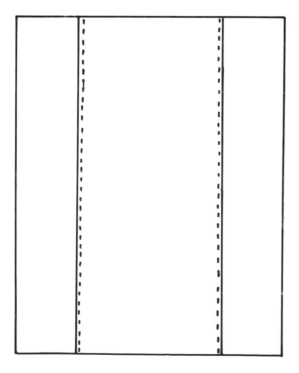

Figure 1. If the quilt top must be pieced, incorporate the piecing into the design. Here, one width of fabric provides the top area. Additional yardage is pieced at two edges of the bed to form side sections, which can be different in color or design.

Opposite page:
Plate 2. "Garden" (detail). Leaves and stems are of colored yarns and heavy floss drawn through from the back of the nylon and tacked, or couched, to the front with mercerized thread.

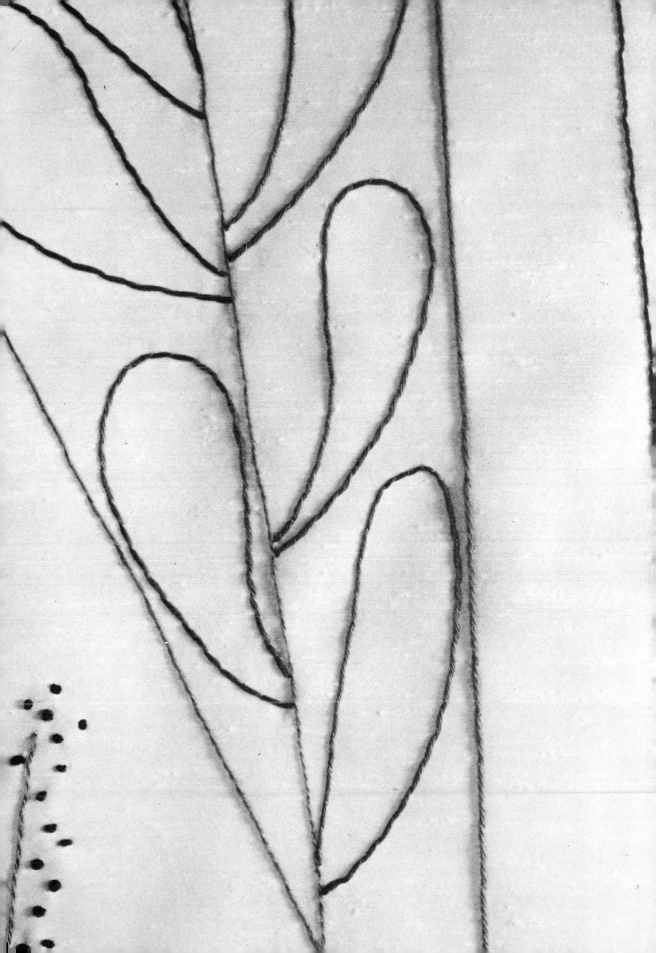

Drawing with Stitches

A single, large piece of material forms the basic top for the coverlet "Garden" (Plate 1). The coverlet is crib-sized and the design was made on a 48-inch-wide fabric. It is a line drawing, using yarn on fabric instead of pencil on paper. The coverlet is easily made and is one which even the beginner could manage.

This kind of line drawing is done with the simple and speedy couching stitch—the yarn is attached to the surface of the top by a second thread, usually mercerized sewing thread. To do this, the yarn is brought through from the back to the front according to the design. In the case of stems, for example, a giant stitch is taken on the front of the fabric so that the yarn is continuous from the bottom of the stem to the very top. The mercerized thread is then drawn through with a second needle and is used to secure the yarn along its length with an overcast stitch or slip stitch. The detail in Plate 2 shows these stitches.

"Garden" is white fabric with stitching in blues, blue-green, and violet. Since the strength of the design relies entirely on a very linear pattern, the contrasts of color can be strong. The leaves as well as the stems are couched yarn, and French knots form the decorative details.

After the top was finished, the backing was made with two pieces of blue cotton broadcloth joined to make a 4-by-6 foot rectangle—the same size as the coverlet top. Then a piece of prewashed cotton flannel was cut to that dimension and placed over the backing material. The couched top was placed on top of these. The three layers were smoothed so that they were wrinkle free, and then they were pinned together. (See Figure 3.)

Figure 2. Yarn is attached (couched) to the fabric top with mercerized thread, forming a line drawing on the material's surface. French knots are made by pulling thread through from back of the material to the front, where it is wrapped around the needle. The needle is drawn through to the back again, pulling the thread into a firm knot.

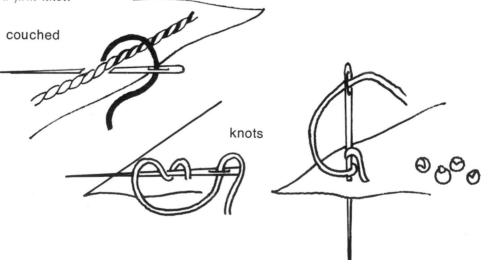

couched

knots

Figure 3. The designed fabric becomes the top layer of the coverlet. A filler is added for the middle layer, and another piece of fabric forms the backing.

Figure 4. French knots provide a decorative treatment to the quilt top and at the same time serve to secure the layers. Each knot is tied on the reverse side of the quilt.

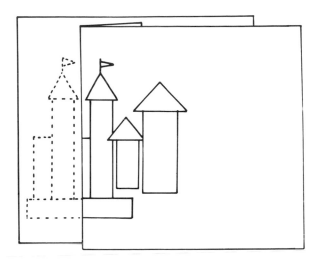

Figure 5. Full-scale drawings on paper may be placed on the fabric top as a guide to stitching the design.

Using three strands of embroidery floss, French knots were made on the coverlet top, with both ends of the floss drawn through to the back layer of the coverlet and tied securely, as shown in Figure 4. Since the layers were tied rather than quilted, "Garden" is considered a coverlet.

The knots used for tying were positioned on the coverlet top at random as they worked into the design. At the upper and lower portions, they occur with some regularity. The knots thus become a part of the overall design as well as the connecting element securing the layers. When knotting and tying were completed, a blanket binding was folded over the raw edges and sewn with running stitches.

The immediacy of couching is exciting, as everything "grows" before your eyes. Anyone who feels uncertain in beginning this way can, of course, work out a drawing in sketch form first. The sketch can be enlarged to full scale on butcher's paper. Avoid putting pencil lines directly onto the fabric since there is a high risk of permanently soiling most fabrics or of having to resort to dry-cleaning for removal of the pencil marks. The enlarged drawing can be folded under and placed next to the quilt top, so that it serves as a guide as you sew each section of the design (Figure 5).

Children's drawings provide excellent subjects for this couching method. Their simplified forms are often charming and especially suitable for quilts.

Another quilt which uses a stitched drawing on a large fabric background is Mark Law's "Sugarplum Tree" in Plate 3. The quilt top is made up of a solid-color cotton fabric. A yard width of the fabric, cut 6 feet long, provides the area for the tree design. Since this was made for a king-size bed, two widths were joined and the design was repeated.

A printed calico was selected for the backing material, and lengths of it were joined to form a backing the same size as the quilt top. A layer of cotton batting was placed over the backing; then the top fabric was laid right side up over the batting. All three layers were pinned together and then basted. Finally, the sugarplum trees were "drawn" onto the material with a needle and thread, using a very small running stitch as the quilting stitch. The stacking of layers and the stitching are described in greater detail in Part III, which discusses the quilting process.

Stitching the design through the layers gives a relief pattern to the quilt top. This method of decorating is, like the couched-yarn technique in the preceding coverlet, an especially good approach for anyone who enjoys drawing. It allows the drawing to provide the overall single design while also providing the quilting pattern. The two emerge as one. A similar effect can be achieved by machine-stitching the design instead of hand-stitching it. A beautiful example of this is shown in Plates 66 and 67 in Part III.

Plate 3. "Sugarplum Tree" by Mark D. Law. Area of each of the two trees is 3' by 6'. Hand-sewn stitches outline the trees and also quilt the layers of material into a single cover with a raised design.

Painting with Batik

"Road Map 5" (Plate 4) by Maureen Nichelson shows a large, abstract design on a single piece of fabric with machine-stitching over it. The abstract form is a batik design on cotton fabric, and suggests a portion of a road map. Providing for a painterly approach to quilt design, batik is a wax-resist method of dyeing a design into the fabric, with the composition worked out in terms of the total area of the quilt top. The desired shapes are painted onto the fabric with melted wax and the entire fabric is dyed. The wax-impregnated areas resist the dye and retain their own color. The process continues with additional waxing and dyeing until the design is complete. Then the wax is removed and the fabric is cleaned and dried.

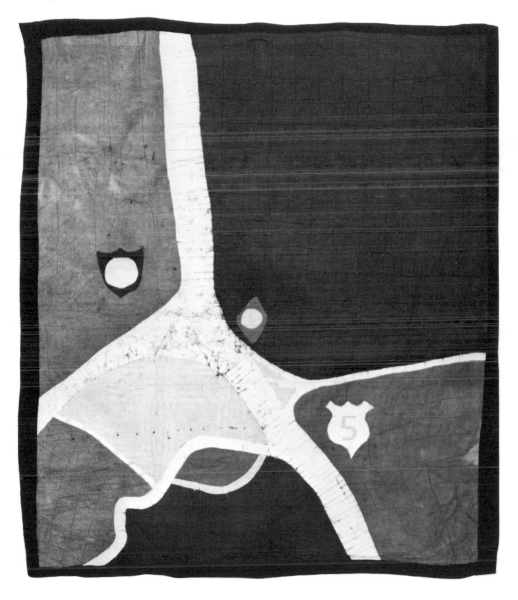

Plate 4. "Road Map 5" by Maureen Nichelson; about 48" by 60". Highways, roads and intersections are described with batik. Quilting stitches, sewn by machine, grow out of the batik forms, adding pattern of a smaller scale to the large shapes.

Plate 5. "Plants Grow" (detail) by Maureen Nichelson. The dye-designed plant forms and lettering are enhanced by delicate line patterns formed in the batik process. Simple machine-stitches serve to quilt layers together.

For this quilt, the completed batik panel was placed over a backing material with a layer of padding between the two. Machine-stitching was used for the quilting pattern which both joins the three layers of fabric and, at the same time, complements the shapes of the batik design. The stitched lines curve and twist, following the lines of the "road" and suggesting adjoining fields and furrows.

Working with batik on a large, single piece of fabric involves an ability to handle the process on a large scale. Using batik on a pieced quilt would be easier for the beginner. An example of pieced batik is in Plates 57 and 58. There are many excellent references on the batik process, and anyone wishing to batik a quilt should study and experiment with the process first.

Maureen Nichelson's mastery of the batik process is seen in a detail from the quilt "Plants Grow" (Plate 5). Her delightful use of lettering, signs, and symbols is a departure in quilt making. The entire quilt pattern and the richness of the batik color appear in Color Plate 20. The quilt's delicate line work, which offers so much textural richness, results from a crackling of the wax. This is controlled by the proportion of paraffin to beeswax in the wax mixture and by the temperature of the wax. Plate 5 shows the beautiful effect of crackling and the very simple lines of the machine-stitched quilting which outlines a band containing the word "grow."

When cotton batting is used as a filler, the quilting stitches must be fairly close so that the batting will be held in place. "Road Map 5" shows quilting which would easily hold the batting. In a quilt like "Plants Grow," however, a woven filler would serve better since the batting can slip out of place when relatively few quilting stitches are used. Woven fillers that work best are pieces of unbleached muslin, cotton "sheet" blankets, and any synthetic or preshrunk blanket. The choice depends upon the need for warmth, the desired weight, and the appearance of the quilt. This will be discussed further in Part III.

Batik with a softer color gradation instead of the linear and more pronounced "crackle" effect is shown in Elizabeth Fuller's appliquéd quilt "A Bedtime Story" (Plate 6). The background fabric and the appliquéd shape are both designed in batik. The marvelous lion's head was painted in wax on a separate fabric and dyed. This batiked form was then cut out and sewn to the large, batiked fabric of the quilt top. The running stitches used for quilting were purposefully related to the shapes in the design. The sunburst at the upper right corner is emphasized by the quilting stitches which repeat the shapes in the batik. On the lion's face, the stitching not only attaches the layers but defines the face as well.

The batik process suggests other means of treating the basic fabric. Designs may be painted onto the quilt top with textile dyes, India ink, or permanent-color felt marking pens. Silk-screen or block printing might be used to embellish the fabric top. Select those ways of working with which you are already familiar and utilize them in your first quilts.

Plate 6. "Bedtime Story" (detail) by Elizabeth Fuller. The lion's head, depicted in batik, was appliquéd to a batiked background. Running stitches emphasize the lion's features and the background design while also serving to quilt the top to a filler and the backing material.

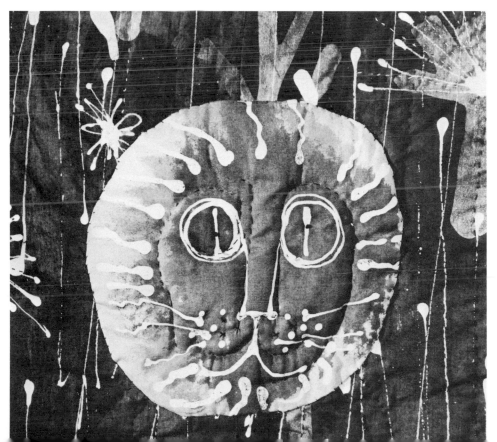

Plate 7. "The Teddy Bear's Blanket" by the author; 25" by 32". Fabric shapes are appliquéd to form a giraffe in a percale jungle of bold prints and brilliant colors.

Appliqué

Starting with the same single, large piece of material, you can apply your design to the quilt top by cutting the shapes you want from various other fabrics and sewing these shapes to the base material in an overall design. In "Teddy Bear's Blanket" (Plate 7) a piece of cotton fabric provides the base material for the coverlet top while the giraffe and the jungle scenery are depicted with cutouts of different fabrics appliquéd directly to the base material. Edges of the appliquéd fabrics are turned under and sewn with a running stitch. The simple running stitch, if knotted carefully at the completion of each sewn line, is remarkably durable and the finished coverlet will withstand a lot of handling. A coverlet such as this, requiring no backing or quilting, can be sewn in a day.

"Flag Quilt" (Plate 8) is also designed with appliquéd forms. Shirl Salzman used a sheet as a base fabric, then pinned her cut shapes to it and basted the pieces in place. After the basting was completed, she took another sheet, placed it over the quilt top, and sewed around three sides. When turned right side out the two sheets formed something similar to a huge pillowcase. Batting was then put between these layers for filler. All three layers were pinned and basted together and the quilting began.

In order to get a quilt this large and bulky under the arm of a sewing machine it was necessary to roll half of it up tightly and sew the exposed half from the center towards the outside edges. The machine-stitching served to appliqué the colors in place as well as to quilt the three layers together.

Plate 8. "Flag Quilt" by Shirl Salzman; about 60" by 72". The puckering and pulling of fabrics adds a liveliness to this velour quilt top. Stitching goes through all layers, applying shapes and quilting them at the same time.

The type of filler selected for the quilt and the materials used for the appliqué are as important as the design. Cotton batting may have to be covered with cheesecloth to help hold it in place. Dacron batting, available in sheet form and similar to cotton batting, is especially nice for quilts. Interested in the tactile qualities, Shirl Salzman likes to use down or feathers for the filler and plush materials for the appliqué. "The whole beauty of a quilt is not only in its design," she says. "Soft corduroys and velours and other 'feely' fabrics are an integral part of quilt making."

"Flag Quilt" is shown in color on page 49. Two other quilts by the same artist are "River Running" (Color Plate 7) and "Landscape" (Plate 9). These quilts also have single-stitched lines serving double duty as appliqué and quilting. This stitching shows in the detail of "Landscape" (Plate 10).

Plate 9. "Landscape" by Shirl Salzman; 54" by 60". Richly varied textures, held by straight machine-stitching, add a tactile appeal to this stuffed and padded quilt.

Plate 10. "Landscape" (detail). Velvet, corduroy, and cotton shapes are all appliquéd, with some larger forms pieced first.

"River Running" (page 53) is a child's quilt and is rich in texture and color. Certainly it is a quilt which would accept the tugging and trampling it would be likely to receive at the hands of a child who loved it and took it everywhere. Part of the quilt's appeal would be in the joy of handling it— the weight, the textures, and the soft, yielding bulk of it.

Prestuffed Quilts

The construction of the quilt "Hills and Valleys" (Plate 11) was especially designed for working with velvet. Ordinarily, velvet is not easy to sew because the pile of the fabric tends to make it slip. This is especially true when two layers are sewn together. This quilt was planned to eliminate some of the difficulty of sewing velvet, while taking full advantage of its textural elegance and tactile appeal.

First a background material that is fairly stiff must be selected and cut to the desired size. A middleweight upholstery fabric, lightweight canvas, heavy cotton twill, pillow ticking, or any other fabric with "body" or some degree of stiffness is suitable. Next, the colors of the velvet design are chosen (see Color Plate 2). You need approximately twice as much velvet as you have background material; that is, for every square yard of finished quilt, you would buy 2 square yards of velvet. From the velvet, cut strips in varying widths, from about 4 inches wide to some which are 10 inches wide. Different colors are joined to form a single strip, and each finished strip should be about 2 inches longer than you actually need to go across the quilt. A random pattern of color change works well, as suggested in Figure 6, or strips can be just one solid color all across.

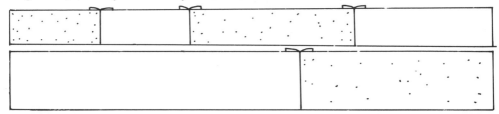

Figure 6. Strips of velvet are cut and joined so that each pieced strip will reach across the width of the quilt.

The first strip of velvet is placed right side down with its lower edge slightly overlapping the top edge of the quilt (Figure 7). The edge of the velvet is pinned and machine-sewn into place with a straight stitch. With the velvet strip still face down, Dacron batting is laid over it along the entire length. The velvet is rolled back over the stuffing, enclosing it. Another row of machine-stitching holds the right side of the velvet in place.

The second strip of velvet is now pinned in position (wrong side up), covering the stitching on the velvet surface of the preceding strip. As you sew, push the first roll back somewhat so that it is out of your way. (Later, it will spring back into position.) Then machine-stitch through both layers of velvet. Since the bottom layer is already sewn in place, you have only the top one to be concerned with. As you progress, the quilt will look like Figure 8.

Figure 7. A line of machine-stitching attaches the first strip of velvet to the base fabric. Dacron batting is used for a stuffing before the other edge is sewn down. The second strip is then placed over the edge of the first.

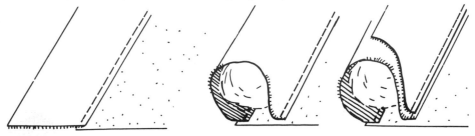

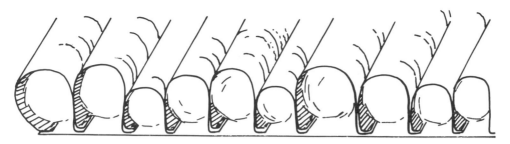

Figure 8. Stuffed strips of velvet form hills and valleys.

By varying the widths of the strips, you vary the height of the rolls. More batting can be added from the ends of the tubular forms, but it is important to have the center of each one well stuffed before going on to the next one. By working from left to right you do not need to be concerned with the bulk, as none of the stuffed forms has to go under the arm of the sewing machine.

When all the strips have been added and stuffed, a lining is sewn to the back. A shiny, bright taffeta was used to line this quilt. Finally, a strip of velvet is used to bind the edges. The tubular forms will need to be flattened with your hand so that you can sew the binding strip over them. The finished quilt is a luxurious combination of color, soft texture and sculptured form.

Plate 11. "Hills and Valleys" (detail) by the author. Strips of velvet, stuffed with Dacron batting, invite you to touch the large, soft and flowing mounds of this simple-to-sew quilt.

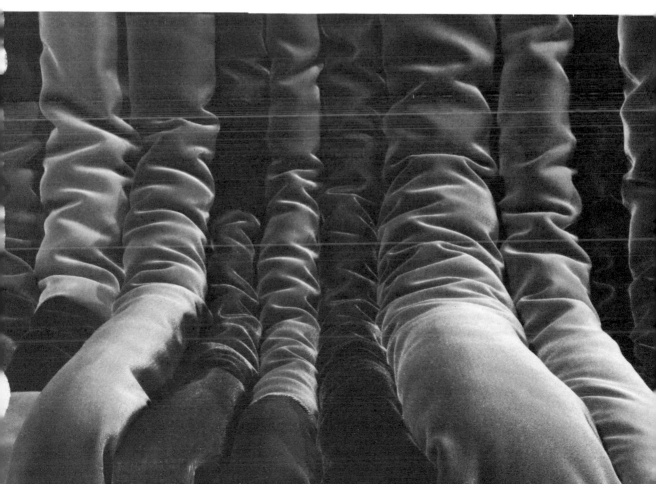

2. Multiple & Repeat Motifs

Instead of providing the quilt top with a single overall motif, you may wish to repeat a design, either in a symmetrical, a random, or an abstract pattern, or to combine several motifs for an overall effect. This treatment of the quilt top produces an effect like that of a collage, and the easiest way to achieve this type of design is to use a series of individual blocks, working on each block or unit separately and sewing each to the large, base material as it is finished. The blocks may be simply cut into different shapes or from different materials, or they may be decorated with appliqué and embroidery or with silk-screen.

"For Sally" (Plate 12) is a coverlet in which a series of blocks is applied directly to a single piece of material. This design, by Anidelle Flint, uses a circular motif repeated in a random pattern over rows of squares. The warmth and brilliance of the colors enhance the total effect (see Color Plate 8).

For any quilt, in determining the necessary yardage, you must first decide on the finished size of the quilt. If, for example, it is 4 feet by 6 feet (a crib size) you would need two 4-foot lengths of 36-inch wide material. It is often helpful to make a sketch to assist you in figuring yardage.

The total for the backing material on a crib-size quilt would be 8 feet, or 2⅔ yards. The appliqué blocks in "For Sally" would require an additional 2⅔ yards, since the entire quilt top is covered with blocks. Material for the circles must also be added. It sometimes helps to purchase an additional ¼ to ½ yard of fabric to give you leeway in arranging the colors.

Once the blocks and the circles are cut, they are laid out in the desired arrangement. The blocks, including those with the circles on them, are then picked up and transferred a few at a time to the quilt top. They are machine-basted into place using a narrow and openly spaced zigzag stitch. More are pinned and basted until the entire top has been covered. After all the shapes are basted in place, a machined satin stitch is used to permanently attach them. Always use a satin stitch wider than the basting stitch so that all threads will be covered. (See Figure 9.)

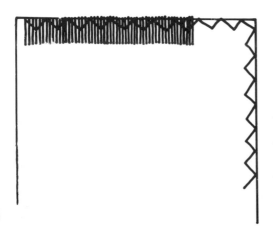

Figure 9. Before appliquéing with a machined satin stitch, first baste the form with a narrow, openly spaced zigzag stitch. Make the satin stitch wide enough to cover all basting stitches.

Plate 12. "For Sally" (detail) by Anidelle Flint. Circles appliquéd to squares with a machine-sewn satin stitch form a repeat-motif pattern. The same stitch attaches the blocks to the backing material.

Plate 13. "Rectangles" (detail) by the author. This sturdy quilt joins overlapping rectangles of cottons to a heavy sailcloth with satin-stitch appliqué.

When blocks or units of the same size are repeated over the entire quilt top, they may be attached so that one shape overlaps the next. In that way, one row of satin stitching holds two edges and it is easier to judge the correct placement of each succeeding block than it is when two separate rows of satin stitching are machine-sewn. An additional allowance of ¼ inch has to be made in the cutting for each edge that overlaps. (See Figure 10.) In machine appliqué, the edges are not turned under; the satin stitch catches any raw edges.

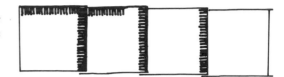

Figure 10. By placing one block so that it overlaps another, you can attach two blocks with one row of stitching.

It may be easier to appliqué the circles to the small blocks before stitching the blocks to the quilt top. However, appliquéing a small area of lightweight material with machine-stitching is apt to cause the material to wrinkle. If your fabric is lightweight, like a cotton broadcloth, an interfacing of iron-on mending tape may be applied to the back of each circle (iron the tape on before cutting the circles), thus making the fabric a bit stiffer and easier to sew. The advantage of stitching the circular appliqués through all the fabric layers is that the pattern of circles then appears on the back of the quilt, along with the pattern of stitching that indicates the horizontal and vertical rows of blocks.

Blocks or geometric shapes can be applied at random as well as in rows. An example is "Rectangles" (Plate 13), one of a pair of unpadded coverlets made for children to use in the back end of a station wagon. The coverlet had to be very strong to withstand the tugging and pulling, so the blocks of rectangles and irregular shapes were applied to a very durable fabric— a heavy sailcloth. Many shapes were cut, of all different sizes, within a close color range. These were reds and oranges, in velour, broadcloth, sateen, and velvet.

Starting in the upper left corner of the quilt, pieces of fabric were machine-stitched directly to the sailcloth. A few shapes at a time were pinned into place, with blocks overlapping so that one row of stitching attached two blocks (Figure 11). This procedure was followed until the sailcloth was entirely covered by a pattern of blocks.

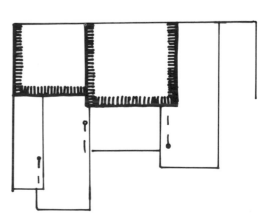

Figure 11. Using random-sized pieces of fabric, overlap them and pin them in place so that one line of stitching attaches more than one block of fabric to the backing.

The block forms can be applied to the backing material with a hand-sewn blind stitch instead of with a machine-sewn satin stitch. The blind stitch gives a fullness and puffiness to the pieces as they are sewn. You can utilize this feature by blindstitching three sides of a block to the backing material and stuffing some Dacron batting into the pocket that is formed. After stuffing the block, sew the last edge with a blind stitch and continue with the next block. All edges must be turned under before they are sewn. In appliquéing small pieces, care must be taken to leave a little fullness in the block. If it is pulled flat and tight there will be no room for stuffing.

Each block is fitted snugly to the one next to it so that eventually the entire surface will be covered. The primary advantage in doing a quilt by this method is that no quilting is required at all. If all knots are hidden and the stitching is done carefully it need not be lined or backed.

Plate 14. "Blues" (detail) by the author. Pieces of fabric are blindstitched to the single-piece top so each forms a pocket. Dacron batting, stuffed inside each pocket of fabric, makes the shapes puff out.

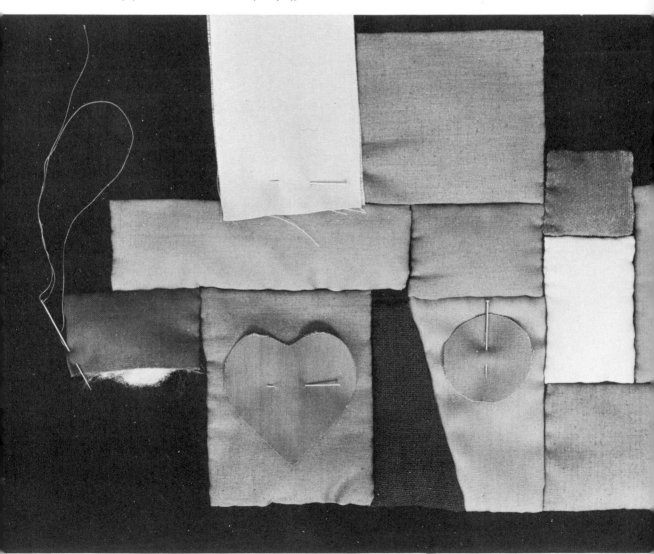

Plate 15. "Dry Creek Quilt" (detail) by the author. Before appliquéd blocks are attached to a fabric backing, cotton flannel is sandwiched beneath each block for filler. Then small running stitches are used for attaching the blocks and for quilting them. Each section is finished individually.

"Blues" (Plate 14) has small geometric shapes, in an assortment of blue cotton fabrics, blindstitched to a single-piece top of washable wool fabric, with each block stuffed as it is applied. This way of working allows for variation. The blocks can be of any size, and the padding can be light or heavy. Appliqué could also be added to the blocks. Some fabric cutouts are shown pinned in place in the photograph; it is easier, however, to appliqué the blocks before applying them to the quilt top.

When finished, a work of this sort has many characteristics of a quilt: there is a fabric top, a padding, and a fabric backing. But it is easy to handle; it requires no quilting stitches to hold the padding and no quilting frame to keep the layers smooth for stitching, so it is an excellent way for the beginning quilt maker to start.

Another simple way to produce a quilt is with hand-appliquéd blocks. A different design can be appliquéd to each block. Once the appliquéd designs are finished, the blocks can be individually lined with cotton flannel filler and sewn to a single-piece top. Each piece of cotton flannel is cut ½ inch smaller in every dimension than the quilt block it is to line. The flannel is then inserted between the quilt block and the backing material, and the raw edges of the block are turned under ¼ of an inch on each side, enclosing the flannel. Then the block is appliquéd in place with a running stitch at the edges of the block (Plate 15). Once the block and its filler are attached, a design can be quilted through all three layers. The quilting stitch should pick up the shapes within the appliquéd block. Note, for example, the stitching that outlines the face of the man in the moon on the corner block in Plate 15.

Plate 16. "Dry Creek Quilt." The quilted blocks are placed so that no spaces show between them. The effect is similar to that of a pieced quilt.

The blocks are placed next to each other so that none of the backing material shows (Plate 16). In this example, all the blocks are based on a 2-inch module; that is, all the blocks are cut in a size that is a multiple of 2 inches. The finished blocks are, therefore, 2 inches by 4 inches, 4 inches by 4 inches, 4 inches by 6 inches, etc. That way, the blocks can always be fitted together. The module can be a multiple of any number. If it were three, the blocks would be 3 inches by 3 inches, 3 inches by 6 inches, etc. Or a single module can be used throughout—all the blocks might be 4 inches by 4 inches, or all could be 3 inches by 6 inches. The module simply provides a basic unit with which to work, one which lends itself readily to repeat.

In cutting the blocks, a ¼-inch seam allowance *must* be made at *each* edge of the block. In working a quilt of this nature, it is a good idea to cut some cardboard patterns both for the blocks and for the flannel lining. A lining block cut 2 inches by 4 inches would be used for a quilt block cut 2½ inches by 4½ inches. When ¼ of an inch was turned under at each edge, the quilt block would measure 2 inches by 4 inches. The cardboard patterns are simple to do and will help you avoid errors, such as forgetting the seam allowance.

The quilt blocks, being small, are a delight to design and sew. The appliqué shapes are deliberately simple, with details added through the embroidery stitches. Plates 17, 18 and 19 show the progression from the cut shapes to the finished, embroidered block. In the first step, fabrics are cut and pinned, with additional fabric allowed for the hemming. In the second, the appliqué with running stitches is almost completed. Finally, embroidery has been added. The "Y" stitch has been used to suggest delicate plants; knots and running stitches form insects.

Right:
Plate 17. Appliquéd quilt block, "Rock" by the author. Design showing a rock surrounded by grass will emerge from simple, cutout forms. Fabrics are cut with an extra ¼ of an inch at each edge.

Below, left:
Plate 18. Quilt block, "Rock." Edges of the cut shapes are turned under and sewn to the fabric block with running stitches.

Below, right:
Plate 19. Quilt block, "Rock." Simple embroidery is added to supply details.

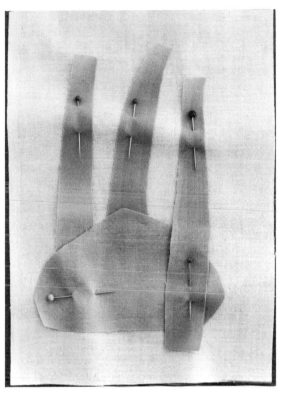

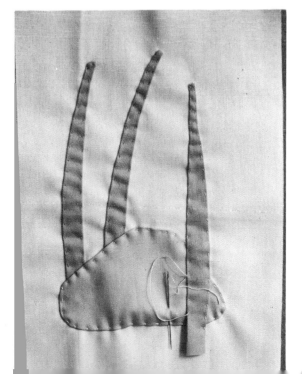

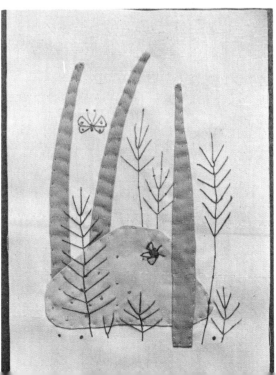

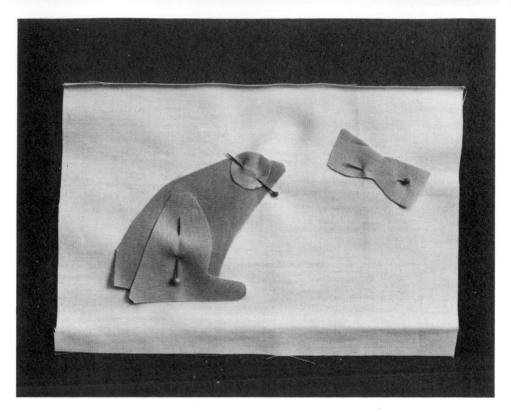

Plate 20. Quilt block, "Frog" by the author. Again the appliqué begins with elemental shapes, this time of a frog and a butterfly, cut from fabric. Cotton broadcloth is used for the shapes and the backing.

Plate 21. Quilt block, "Frog." The completed block, enhanced by stitching, is sewn in place on the quilt top. The edges of the block have been turned under, enclosing the edges of the flannel. Quilting stitches outline the frog and create a border inside the block.

In another pair of examples (Plates 20 and 21), the frog is seen first in simply cut shapes, pinned into place. Then it is shown after being appliquéd, embroidered and, finally, added to the quilt.

A quilt made with these lined blocks has the features of a standard quilt. It is padded, it has a quilting pattern, and the quilting carries through to the back. Like the preceding quilt "Blues," the primary advantage is that the quilt is finished as you go along; it is never necessary to handle the entire quilt to do the quilting.

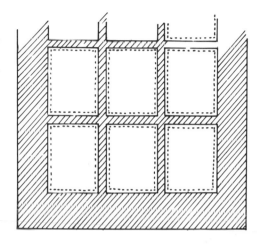

Figure 12. The background need not be entirely covered. Blocks can be appliquéd to a quilt top of contrasting color with spaces left between the blocks as part of the design.

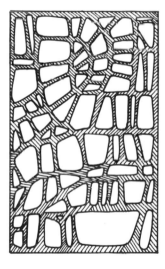

Figure 13. Abstract shapes can also be appliquéd so that the background is incorporated into the design. Each shape here is cut to repeat or echo the shapes next to it.

Blocks can also be applied so that portions of the background are allowed to show as part of the design. "Pomegranates" has off-white blocks containing brilliant red pomegranates distributed over a bright red, Mexican cotton top (Plate 22). The basic pomegranate shape on each block was printed by silk-screen. An iron-on tape (Plate 23) forms the seeds within the pomegranate, with no two being treated quite the same. Using these methods makes it possible to produce a quilt depicting a specific idea, with detail, in a very speedy and simple way. Each block is sewn on separately and then a quilting stitch outlines each fruit, further attaching the block to the background. That is all of the sewing involved, except for the French knots at the base of each fruit.

Plate 22 shows the progression of the block designs. The bottom row has a block that is silk-screened only. The next two are screened and sewn, and have iron-on tape added. The blocks above have the knots and the detailed quilting already finished.

Iron-on tape will withstand a few washings, though eventually some of the seed cutouts will probably have to be replaced. That simply means ironing on a new shape. Iron-on tape may not be the best material from which to make a quilt, but for those situations when time is of a greater essence than the lasting qualities of the quilt, it will certainly help. If your child is currently interested in beetles, or constellations, or space ships, the iron-on tape makes it possible to do a coverlet with that specific design and to finish it before his interests have changed.

Because iron-on tape is not sewn it will not have the textural quality of the appliquéd pieces. But it is a good solution for those tiny hard-to-sew shapes. In making a quilt which I intended for my own use or intended to be used for years, I would not use the iron-on tape. If, however, a child requested a quilt with many particular details, and iron-on tape made that possible, I would use it. A single line of machine-stitching would help assure more permanence in the application of the tape.

Plate 22. "Pomegranate" (detail) by the author. This series of blocks shows the progression from a silk-screened design (bottom row, left) to the finished blocks (top row) with iron-on tape, quilting stitches and French knots added. Blocks are spaced so that red background material is incorporated into the overall design.

Plate 23. "Pomegranate" (finished detail). Silk-screen printing produced the scarlet pomegranate shape, and iron-on tape was used to detail the seeds. The outlining in bright red thread is a running stitch.

Silk-screening has great potential for quilt making. It is a stencil method of printing, and can be accomplished most simply with paper cutouts. I used paper stencils under the silk-screen frame for the pomegranate design. Screening makes it possible to use very detailed design and lettering. Very little has been done with quilting and screened blocks, though a few people have begun to work with it. It is not new, of course, as there are many old English and American quilts which used block printing on the fabrics for basic design, and the quilting was then developed around the prints. In Chapter 3 there is an example of silk-screen printing on felt. Any kind of block printing is excellent for repeating a single motif in an overall pattern.

A design that uses many variations of one motif is Stephanie Cyr's intriguing "Quilted Coverlet" (Plate 24), which has a marvelous array of fabrics, ribbons, crocheting, rickrack, and portions of printed lettering on cloth. It is a nostalgic collection, suggesting and hinting at things of the past. The pieces are sewn with both hand- and machine-stitching. Plate 25 shows a detail of the various textures. The torn fabric fringes are a wonderful addition for the way in which they move when the quilt is handled.

The printed designs on feed bags and cloth sacks are fine sources for quilt blocks. One quilt I know of was made from old flour and sugar sacks.

Opposite page:
Plate 24. "Quilted Coverlet" by Stephanie Cyr; 36" by 60". Printed fabrics, ribbons, crocheted work, edgings, and lace mingle together in this intriguing quilt, which is reminiscent of the past but contemporary in concept.

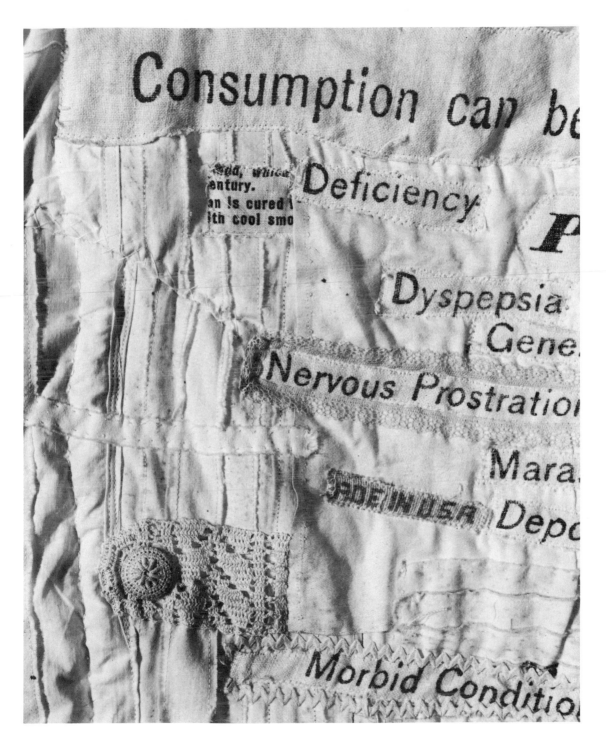

Plate 25. "Quilted Coverlet" (detail). Bold patterns of lettering contrast with fine textures of lace and tatting. Both machine-sewing and hand-stitching are used.

Plate 26. "Labels" (detail) by the author. Collected from coats, sweaters, and dresses, labels provide a colorful source of "prefinished blocks" for an appliquéd coverlet.

Another, which was described to me, was made by a woman who helped her husband run a general store years ago in the "Mother Lode" country. The storekeeper's wife picked up all the discarded Bull Durham tobacco bags and used the decorative front design for her quilt blocks.

There seem to be fewer printed fabrics of this nature available nowadays. Somehow using the authentic printing from a sugar bag is much more interesting than buying printed yardage. Along with the charm of these old prints, the delightful, added touch of making something from almost nothing is lost. One form of lettered fabric still available to us is in the form of modern-day labels from clothing. Plate 26 shows the beginning of a coverlet using these woven labels.

The labels are sewn to a solid-colored backing fabric using a running stitch. When enough labels are collected they offer some color selection, so that areas of a coverlet can run to greens, blues or reds. The backs of labels have much more color, but the loose threads might cause some problems in catching or fraying. The labels provide you with a prefinished block, often having bound or woven edges, so that you need only arrange the blocks and stitch them in place. Small pieces of solid colors could be intermixed to complement the areas of lettering.

Another means of working with multiple design units on a single-piece top is to start with a ready-made cover. A sheet or a solid-colored bedspread would do. The material should be fairly smooth-woven.

Plate 1. "Flag Quilt" by Shirl Salzman; 60" by 72". Brilliantly colored velvets were appliquéd with machine-stitching which also holds the soft padding in place.

Plate 2. "Hills and Valleys" by the author; 54" by 54". Strips of velvet filled with Dacron batting form a sculptured surface.

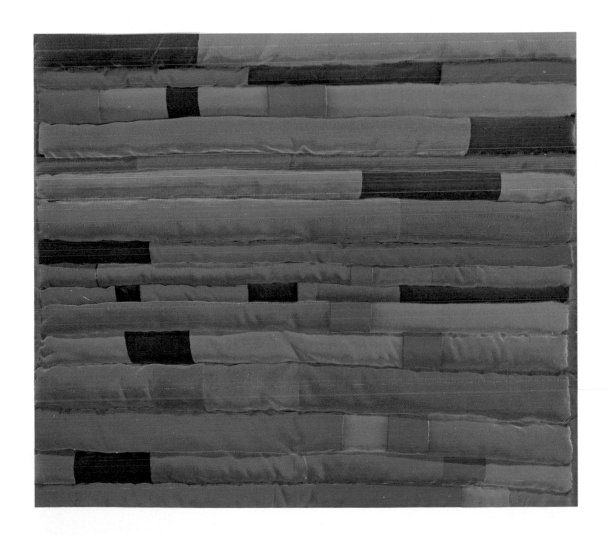

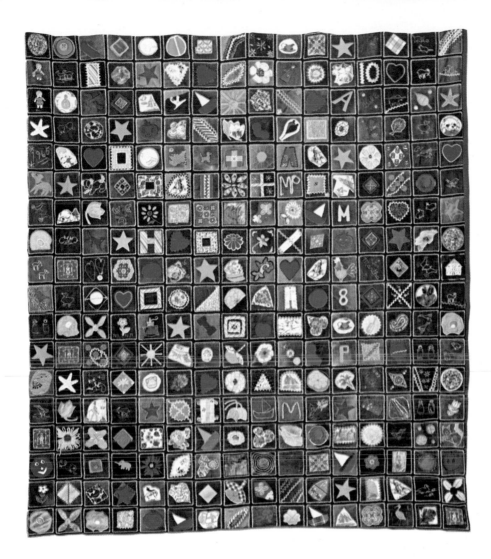

Plate 4. "Denim Quilt," 56" by 72". Of faded-denim blocks and cotton appliqué, this is the collective work of women from the Third Ward Relief Society, the Church of Jesus Christ of Latter-Day Saints, in Oakland, California.

Plate 5. "Friendship Quilt" by Susan Ruettgers and friends; 74" by 90". The fabric blocks are appliquéd, then pieced together in vertical rows that are joined to form the quilt top.

Plate 6. "American Dream" by Lynn Learned Sims; 72" by 90". A pieced rainbow of bright cotton strips is overlaid with a large appliquéd form. The black borders overhang the top of a queen-sized bed.

Plate 7. "River Running" by Shirl Salzman; 40" by 48". Strong textures and vibrant colors add warmth to this thickly padded quilt.

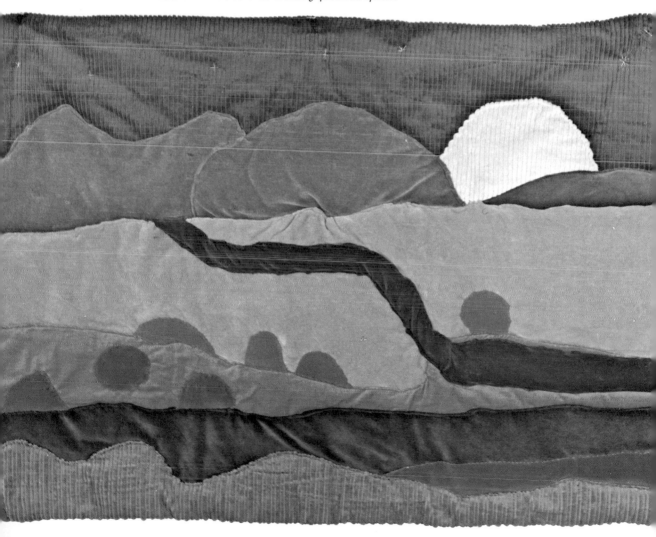

Plate 8. "Lizabeth's Quilt" by the author; 34" by 50". Cotton appliqués on cotton blocks pieced in repeat pattern form the basic design in the crib quilt.

Plate 9. "For Sally" (detail) by Anidelle Flint. Simple squares and circles are combined in this machine-appliquéd quilt.

Plate 11. "Quilt Block" (detail) by the author; 4" by 4" block from quilt below. A simple running stitch is used for both the appliqué and quilting stitch.

Plate 12. "Child's Quilt" by the author; 40" by 50". Simple appliqué forms are repeated in various colors on cotton blocks joined by piecing. Photographed through the courtesy of Farm Journal.

Plate 13. "Tom's Quilt" by the author; 50" by 74". Based on a patchwork approach, this quilt uses appliqué designs on blocks of all shapes and sizes.

Plate 14. "Les Fleurs Vives" by June O'Neill; 74" by 90". Blocks based on a modular unit make this richly colored quilt easy to assemble.

Plate 17. "Pillow Quilt" (detail) by the author. Prefinished "pillow" forms are stitched together in a quilt that is finished as you go.

Plate 18. "Quilt" (detail) by Charles Counts and the Rising Fawn Quilters. Appliquéd cottons are combined with the delicate line drawings of the quilting.

Plate 19. "Quilt" (detail) by Charles Counts and the Rising Fawn Quilters. Appliqué and quilting are beautifully integrated as the stitching pattern tends to grow out of the appliquéd forms.

Plate 20. *"Plants Grow" by Maureen Nichelson; 66" by 74". The batik design yields a finely detailed coverlet.*

Plate 21. (detail of the work below). Stitching diversifies the scale of the design and adds another dimension to it.

Plate 22. "Quilt" by Charles Counts, about 72" by 90". This quilt, contemporary in design, retains the integrity and beauty of fine and carefully planned quilting.

Plate 23. "La Chola en La Colcha" by Joan Lintault; 86" by 104". Traditional block designs are used as a point of departure in this modern quilt. The figure is stuffed and padded and appears to be both under the quilt and growing out from the surface.

Plate 24. "Bridget Quilt" by Therese McMahan May; 76" by 90". Combined here are the elements of a traditional quilt with the photographic-image approach of contemporary painting.

A sheet offers a good base for a lightweight, summer coverlet. By buying a sheet larger than what would ordinarily be needed on the bed, you will have plenty of fabric coming over the sides. For example, a full-size sheet used on a single bed provides a top that comes nearly to the floor on each side. A king-size sheet on a double bed works the same way. Check the exact size of your bed, as well as height off the floor. Check sheet sizes. On a king-size bed, it would be necessary to have two single-size sheets— one for the top area, and one to split to form the sides.

Once the top sheet is ready, place it on the bed. Then cut your designs and shapes from cotton fabrics and lay them in place. Pre-appliquéd blocks may be used instead and sewn onto this kind of backing. Large, simple, geometric shapes are most easily appliquéd to a sheet with machine-stitching. Hand-sewing would be preferable for any curved or complex shapes. Figure 14 shows some possibilities for appliquéing directly to a sheet.

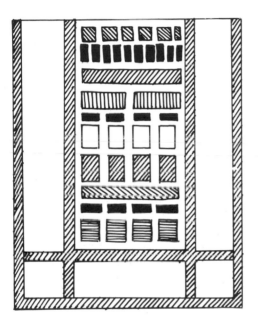

Figure 14. Bed sheets provide excellent backing for lightweight coverlets. Use machine-stitching to appliqué straight-edged forms. Stitch circles and curves by hand or by a machined satin stitch.

Should you wish to make a quilt rather than a coverlet, simply use another sheet of the same size for backing, and select your filler or padding. Cotton "sheet" blankets make good lightweight filler. For a heavier quilted effect, use a sturdier top fabric, such as a tightly woven, ready-made cotton spread, in place of the sheet. To this top you can attach small, prestuffed, shingle-like shapes. (See Figure 15.) The shapes will be sewn on in horizontal rows so that each succeeding row overlaps the previous one like the shingles on a roof.

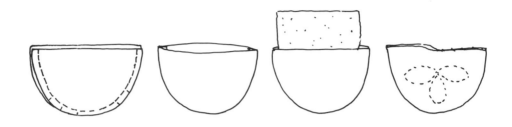

Figure 15. Shingles or petals of fabric can be cut and sewn, then turned and stuffed. A simple quilting design holds the three layers together. The open end is then turned under and slip-stitched closed to complete the flap shape.

First select the bedspread that provides your base. Measure the overall width to determine how many blocks of what size will fill one row. Suppose the backing is 72 inches wide. If you use a finished block of 4 inches, you need 18 blocks across one row. If you use a 6-inch block, then you need 12 of them for one row; using an 8-inch block, you would need 9 blocks for each row. Just make sure that the width of your quilt top can be divided evenly by the width of the individual block.

Next you start making these individual shapes. They may be thought of as petal shapes. Each one is cut from a double layer of fabric and sewn with the end left open so it can be turned and stuffed. Once a series of these shapes is turned, stuffed, and quilted, you are ready to assemble them.

A row of the prefinished "shingles" is placed on the spread and pinned in position. Start with the very bottom row, so that subsequent rows overlap. This overlapping is shown in Figure 16. The first row is then sewn down with a line of straight machine-stitching. On the next row, a half-shingle has to be used at each edge. These are most easily made half the size of the other shingles at the time that they are cut.

The second row is now pinned in place overlapping the first one, and it is sewn to the backing. When all the rows are finished, the spread assumes the form of a quilt. If your shingle shapes are long (over 6 inches), you may need to tack down the end of an occasional one, especially at the quilt's sides, to keep them from flapping. Shorter ones will stay in place more easily. You can also limit the covered area to the top or flat portion of the bed, reserving enough shingles to make a border at the bottom edge.

Using any of the methods shown in this chapter is a good way for the beginner to learn quilting. Applying blocks is a system that remains suitable whether your preference is for hand-sewing or machine-sewing, for solid colors or appliqué, for preprinted fabrics or hand-screened blocks. This way of working is so versatile that even the most skilled and experienced quilter will find it absorbing. It may take time to accumulate enough appliquéd blocks, or labels, or printed words to fill a quilt, but with this approach it doesn't seem to matter. You continue to collect and sew, and when your supply is adequate, you appliqué the blocks to a top. In the total collection, each block is enhanced by the others.

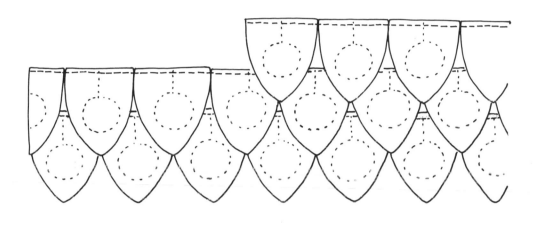

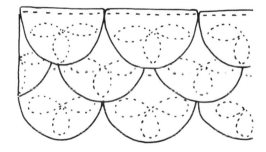
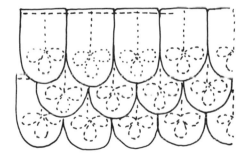

Figure 16. Machine-stitching is used to attach these petal shapes, one row at a time, to a ready-made bedspread. Petals or shingles can vary in size and shape as shown. Every other row will have a half-block at each edge, while alternate rows have whole blocks.

3. Felt Appliqué

Felt, in its beautiful array of colors, can be used to make a brilliant and stunning coverlet or quilt. The primary disadvantage to its use is that the material must be dry-cleaned. It cannot be laundered. But this is true of many other fabrics used for bedspreads and should not discourage the use of felt. If felts are bought through a decorator, which is the best source for specific colors, they can be ordered pretreated by a Scotchgard process. Some cleaning establishments will also pretreat felt. It would be helpful to have the felt material made stain-resistant through this process. Though most surface dust can be tumble-dried out or shaken off, if the felt gets badly soiled, it will probably have to be cleaned. Automatic dry-cleaning machines make this simple and inexpensive.

Felt is easy to sew through, and the edges need not be turned under. Because the cut edge is the finished edge, felt can be used for small forms and complex shapes or letters that would otherwise be almost impossible to appliqué if the edges had to be turned. The felt can be appliquéd directly to the backing material in an overall design or to separate blocks of material which are then stitched to the backing.

The "Cherry Tree" coverlet in Plate 27 is a single-motif design of felt appliqué on hopsacking. The white area covers the top of a single bed, with colored panels used at the sides and foot of the bed. The tree, leaves, and cherries are all appliquéd to the top by means of a running stitch. A detail (Plate 28) shows these stitches along the edges of the felt.

Any fabric that has enough weight and body to support the felt can be used as the backing material. This includes Indian head and denim as well as hopsacking. When the top and sides are made with different-colored panels, either part can be emphasized as the primary area of design. Figure 17 gives some suggestions on handling single-motif appliqué.

Plate 27. "Cherry Tree" by the author; area of tree is 3' by 6½'; total quilt is 6½' by 8'. Red, pink, and orange cherries of brilliant felts are applied to a hopsacking background in a single-motif design.

Plate 28. "Cherry Tree" (detail). Simple running stitches hold the edges of the felt. Material will not ravel and edges do not have to be turned under.

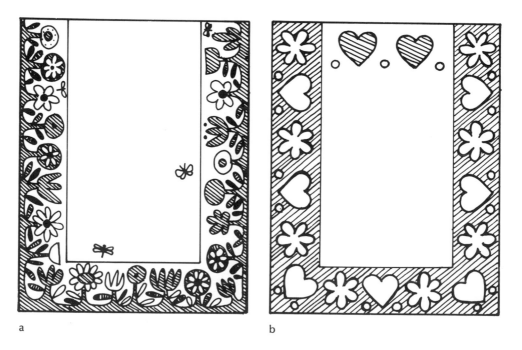

a   b

Figure 17. Emphasis in the overall design can be given to either the top area or the side panels of a quilt. In sketches **a** and **b** emphasis is given to the sides, with the top area repeating one of the colors in the appliqué. In **c** and **d** the design emphasis is on the top of the quilt. A contrasting color could be used on the side panels.

c   d

In an example of an appliquéd block (Plate 29), a running stitch was used to appliqué the dove, wings, leaves, and feathers; French knots were used on the eye and heart. Either stitch works well; it is simply a matter of preference. The running stitch goes faster, though the detail of the knots is decorative and confetti-like. Some of the knots have moved off the appliqué so that they are essentially embroidered details. The felt pieces were appliquéd to a block of coarsely woven material so there is a contrast of textures; the threads in the backing panel subtly offset the smooth-surfaced felt.

Plate 29. Quilt block, "Dove" by the author. Felt shapes appliquéd to a block of coarsely woven material provide textural contrast. Running stitches hold the felt in place; French knots are used for decorative detail.

Plate 30. Block design, "Hearts" by the author. Heart shapes are silk-screened onto felt blocks. French knots at the edges appliqué the blocks, and embroidery stitches create various leaf designs within the hearts.

Silk-screened blocks of felt were appliquéd to a felt background for the quilt in Plate 30. In the upper left corner of the photograph there is a block with a simple screened form. It is in red paint and lets the felt color come through as the heart. The blocks were in an assortment of colors, including yellow, yellow-green, and pink. The screened blocks were embroidered in the centers, using two strands of embroidery floss to suggest ferns and flowers. Then the blocks were appliquéd by using a series of French knots at the outside edge. A second row of knots, while not essential to hold the block in place, adds a delicate edge to the bold heart shape. The blocks are sewn to a felt background. Felt, because it comes in 72-inch widths, provides a good material for the single-piece backing.

A similar design of heart shapes could be accomplished without silk-screening. The felt shapes could be cut from different colors and stacked to arrive at several different effects (Figure 18). In each of these stacks, additional rows of stitching would be required to attach the edge of the smaller square and of the heart shape. There are always numerous ways of working out any one design idea. Just select the one that works best for you, depending upon the intended use of the finished piece and your own sewing abilities.

Figure 18. Felts can be cut and stacked to produce designs. In the top row, a red square, then a white square, and finally a red heart are stacked. In the bottom row, a white square is covered by a smaller red square, out of which the heart shape has been cut.

Pennye Kurtela's coverlet in Plate 31 consists of a series of felt rectangles in the standard available size, 9 inches by 12 inches, appliquéd with felt tree shapes. The colors alternate between blue and white. Here all the blocks are sewn to a single, large piece of felt. Most felts which are 50 per cent wool will be durable enough for the quilt top. All of the appliqué in this coverlet is done with French knots, which add a decorative sparkle and a detail to the design. The variations on the tree form continue through the coverlet.

Plate 31. "Trees" (detail) by Pennye Kurtela. Felt blocks are appliquéd and stitched to a felt background with French knots. Blocks of blue and white alternate.

Figure 19. Numbers and letters, ordinarily difficult to appliqué, can easily be cut from felt and sewn to blocks. The letters can be cut to leave space at the edges of the block, or they can be cut so that the letter touches the edges.

Figure 20. Using the traditional block form and a repeat unit, there are infinite possibilities in felt. Intricate shapes and sharp points are easily appliquéd because the raw edge does not have to be turned under.

A further use for felt is in alphabet blocks. Letters, because of the inside curves and corners, are difficult to appliqué in most fabrics. Figure 19 suggests a possible way of doing a quilt using felt alphabet blocks. The letters can be appliquéd first; then the finished block can be sewn to a background piece. The blocks could be stuffed or padded, though the felt itself has a certain amount of thickness which will add weight to the finished block. Some more ideas for felt block designs are shown in Figure 20. These motifs could also be carried out in cotton appliqué or in silk-screen.

Plate 32. "Orbiting Garden" (detail) by Pennye Kurtela. A sheet of felt provides the single-piece top, onto which smaller cutouts are sewn with overcasting.

"Orbiting Garden" (Plate 32) shows a detail of a felt quilt in which a single, large, felt piece forms the base. No identical blocks are repeated, but variations of circular shapes are sewn directly to the background. Overcast stitches add a prickly, active edge, especially where thread and felt colors contrast strongly. The collection of similar shapes—circles, circular flowers, and cutout circles—produces an integrated, overall pattern.

Felt should not be considered inappropriate as a possible material for coverlets or quilts. It is not a traditionally accepted material for quilts, but only recently have these good quality felts been so available at reasonable prices and in such a beautiful array of colors. With coin-operated dry-cleaning, the care of felt is not a problem. Because felts are so easily worked with, they provide an excellent material for anyone about to venture into quilt making for the first time.

Part II

PIECED TOPS

Pieced tops are those that are designed and formed by joining a collection of many smaller pieces of fabrics. This mosaic-like piecing can produce pictorial, abstract, or geometric designs arranged in either symmetrical or random patterns. In all cases, the decorative design and the structure form an integral unit. Each part is dependent on the other and the result of the deceptively simple piecing process is visually complex.

Pieced tops may utilize patterns of available solid colors and printed fabrics, or they may result from the joining of personally designed fabric pieces such as appliquéd blocks or home-dyed cloths. For anyone who feels hesitant about drawing, the piecing together of abstract patterns or geometric forms may have special appeal. The limitless possibilities for variation in arranging colors and shapes offer the exciting prospect of producing a quilt that is both personal and unique in its design.

Plate 33. "Lizabeth's Quilt" (detail) by the author. Decorated squares are pieced together. Edges of appliquéd shapes are turned under and sewn with a running stitch on each block. The blocks are then sewn together vertically and horizontally to form the top. A layer of filler and a backing are added and the top is quilted with running stitches inside each block.

1. Joining Appliqué Blocks

The simplest piecing is accomplished through the joining of the simplest forms. If all the blocks are the same size, then certainly they are more easily put together. The blocks in "Lizabeth's Quilt" (Plate 33) were all cut to finish at 3 inches square. This means that all the blocks would fit together no matter how they were arranged.

In making a pieced quilt of squares, the colors must first be determined. For this quilt, varying shades of blues and lavenders were selected. All blocks were cut 3½ inches square, allowing ¼ of an inch at each edge for the seam. The designs for appliqué (the circles and leaves) were then cut from the same assortment of colors as the blocks and they were appliquéd onto the blocks. By alternating between two designs, you need the same number of each one to make up the entire top. Appliqué of this kind is very simple. The task of drawing is limited to making the circle and one leaf. Beyond that, the designing is a matter of arranging colors.

The best procedure is to first appliqué the designs onto each of the individual blocks. The appliquéd blocks are then laid out on the table, or any other flat surface, to determine the arrangement. The blocks are picked up in that order and joined to one another vertically with a running stitch (Figure 21). These are sewn by hand, though machine-sewing would also work since all blocks are cut on the straight of the material. One row of blocks is completed, then another, so that the two rows can be joined horizontally. The rows are placed with the right sides together, and are pinned and sewn (Figure 22).

Hand-sewing the blocks assures a better fit at corners because it allows you to adjust the fabric as you sew. The other advantage to hand-sewing is that you can take blocks with you and work on the sewing wherever you happen to be. It is not necessary to go to the sewing machine to do your work. In piecing squares or rectangles, however, machine-stitching is quicker.

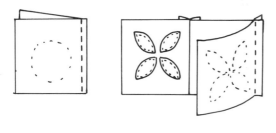

Figure 21. Appliqué blocks are joined to one another vertically, using a straight or running stitch. Enough are joined to form a row the width of the quilt. Seams are pressed open.

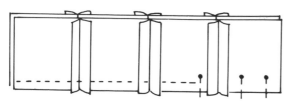

Figure 22. Finished rows are pinned face to face, then sewn together horizontally, either by hand- or by machine-sewing.

Plate 34. "Apples" (cutouts for quilt blocks) by the author. A simple idea may be repeated over and over, offering variations in color, shape, or arrangement. One apple may be whole, another a cross section.

The blocks for pieced and appliquéd quilts are always finished first, and then sewn together. Any smoothly woven fabric, as broadcloth or percale, works well. Some of the all-synthetic fabrics may work, but they often have quite a bit of "spring" to them and are sometimes harder to turn under and sew.

The blocks in Plate 34 have apple shapes that are cut and ready to be pinned and sewn. By the time all edges on the stems, leaves, and apples are turned under, the shapes will be much smaller, allowing room for seams at the sides of the blocks. All shapes for appliqué must be cut large enough so that the loss of ⅛ to ¼ of an inch in the hem does not change the design you want (Figure 23). The smaller the shapes on which you work, the greater the difference that this turned-under hem will make. Edges that are to be covered by another shape need not be turned under (Figure 24). A tree trunk partially covered by a foliage shape, for example, need be sewn only at the sides and at the bottom. To sew the top edge, also, would add unnecessary bulk and extra sewing. The edge will lie flatter if left unsewn.

hemmed

Figure 23. Cut fabric shapes for the appliquéd design large enough to allow for a hem. The dashed line indicates the hemming allowance and finished size of an apple and leaf appliqué.

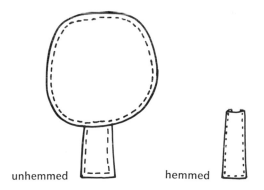

unhemmed   hemmed

Figure 24. Turn and sew only the edges of the appliqué that will be exposed. Where shapes overlap it is not necessary to hem the edge that is covered, as in the top edge of this tree trunk covered by foliage.

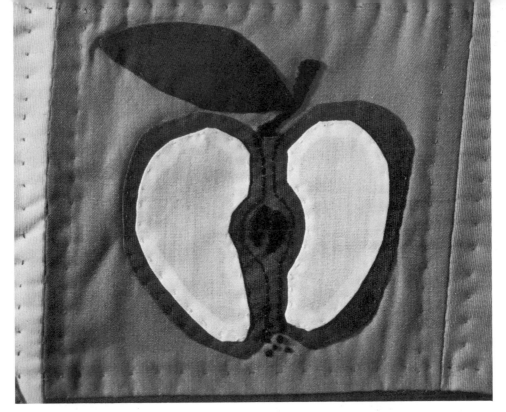

Plate 35. "Apple" (quilt block). Finished block has been appliquéd, joined to the other blocks and quilted. In appliquéing the shapes, larger pieces of fabric are easier to handle than tiny ones. Sew the largest shape to the quilt block first, adding other appliqué forms and embroidery details last.

Plate 36. "Child's Quilt" by the author; 40" by 50". Several different designs, including the apple, are used repeatedly, though in various colors, to produce the overall pattern.

The apple block in Plate 35 is a detail from "Child's Quilt" (Color Plate 12). The primary apple shape is cut first, and sewn to the block; then the smaller inside pieces are sewn on top through the three layers of fabric. The stem is embroidered, as are the seeds, since those shapes were too small to appliqué. This detail also shows the quilting stitch which outlines each block in the "Child's Quilt." A larger portion of the quilt appears in Plate 36. This quilt is made on a modular unit of 4 inches. All blocks finish at 4 by 4 inches or 4 by 8 inches. That way, they fit together to form a rectangle. Some of the 4-by-8 inch blocks are used vertically and some horizontally. There are ten different designs, repeated in varying color combinations.

In planning such a quilt, the modular unit is established and the color range selected. (Here, greens, blue-greens, white, and yellow were used.) The blocks are cut, adding ¼ of an inch at each edge for seam allowance. Then the appliqué is added to the blocks. These small areas of stitchery are a delight to do—each is easily handled, and one block can be finished in a short time, so there is a growing feeling of accomplishment. Some of the blocks are left solid, with no appliqué.

Plate 37. Quilt block, "Turtle" by the author. Forms found in nature provide ideas for designs. Shapes representing a turtle are appliquéd to a cotton broadcloth block with a simple running stitch. A single strand of embroidery floss is used for grass and weeds.

Plate 38. Quilt block, "Moth" by the author. The moth is a simple design from just two pieces of fabric. French knots add to the details.

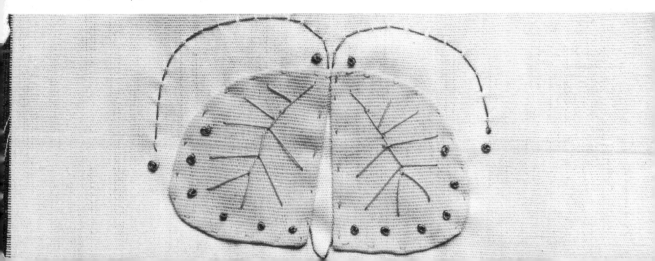

Jane O'Neill's "Les Fleurs Vives" (Color Plate 14) uses blocks 5 by 5 inches and 5 by 10 inches, assembled after the appliqué was finished. These blocks are joined by a running stitch. If you machine-sew, be sure to tie threads at both ends. In hand-sewing, knot your thread to start with and take a catch stitch at the other end.

"A Boy's Quilt" (Plate 39) uses a constant 10-inch height for all blocks, letting the widths vary. This allows for blocks of almost any size, up to 10 inches high, and yet keeps the assembly very simple. Some blocks were cut less than 10 inches high and were joined to a piece of solid or printed fabric so that the finished size was still 10 inches (Figure 25). The blocks were joined into horizontal bands until the desired width of the quilt was achieved; then the assembly was simply a matter of joining horizontal bands until the desired length of the quilt was reached. A solid brown and a brown print were used to alternate with the appliquéd blocks. This was a large quilt, 72 inches by 90 inches, and to assure my finishing it before my son had outgrown it, the addition of plain blocks was a great help.

The blocks for the "Friendship Quilt" (Color Plate 5) were joined into vertical bands first instead of horizontal ones. This quilt was assembled and finished by Susan Ruettgers, who received many of the blocks for it at a shower given in honor of the impending arrival of her baby. Socorro Kimble planned the quilt by selecting the colors and precutting all the rectangles.

Figure 25. Using appliqué and plain or printed material, blocks of all sizes can be combined in bands, as long as a maximum height is determined first. The variation in size and shape of the blocks adds to their "patchwork" appearance.

Plate 40. "Ant House," a quilt block by Susan Ruettgers; detail of Color Plate 5. Susan appliquéd and embroidered the design based on a drawing by her son.

Plate 41. "Flower," a quilt block by Bess Elliott; detail of Color Plate 5. Appliquéd flowers ornament this quilt block of cotton fabrics made for a pieced quilt.

These precut blocks were sent out with the party invitations and with a request that they be appliquéd and returned to Susan. The variety is remarkable and, because of the planning in terms of sizes and colors, the assembly was simplified and the total effect charming. Anyone planning such a quilt would find it helpful to designate whether blocks were to be hand-sewn or machine-sewn, and whether or not names and dates were to be included.

Details of two of the blocks from "Friendship Quilt" are shown in Plates 40 and 41. The cross section of an ant hill was from a drawing by Susan Ruettger's son Kenny. In the Color Plate, at the lower edge of the quilt, you can see a snowman which was drawn by another son, Steve.

Color Plate 13 of "Tom's Quilt" shows a quilt top pieced from irregular-shaped blocks. There is no modular unit or repeat. The piecing is more difficult and the overall effect more complex.

The blue denim quilt in Plate 42 is pieced from almost 300 small blocks joined together with black-yarn crochet. Because of the number of different small designs, the overall pattern takes on a rich complexity. Some squares are merely covered with rickrack or smaller squares of fabric. Others are embroidered and appliquéd. Cutout prints, bits of stitching and decorative edgings are all used.

Plate 42. "Denim Quilt" by members of the Third Ward Relief Society, the Church of Jesus Christ of Latter-Day Saints, Oakland, California; detail of Color Plate 4. Numbers, letters, abstract forms, geometric shapes and everyday objects are depicted on the blocks of blue denim, which were joined by crocheting.

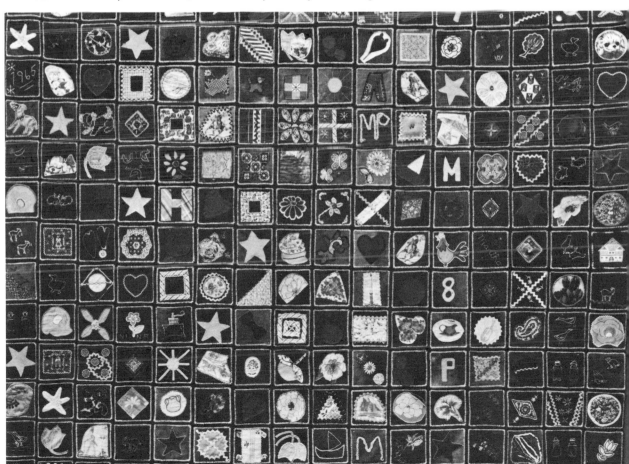

Plate 43. "Bunnies" by the author. The blocks are appliquéd so that three of them form one design element. The shapes are machine-sewn to the blocks, which are then pieced together in the predetermined pattern. You can also appliqué the shapes after the blocks have been joined.

Blocks to be pieced into a quilt need not always be appliquéd by hand. Machine appliqué will work provided there is enough body or weight to the fabric so that it won't pucker from the machine-sewing. The repeat block can suggest the basic pattern with simple appliqué over that. Plate 43 shows the basic block arrangement for "Bunnies." The blocks were appliquéd before they were joined together. Hand-embroidered details were added later with couched lines and French knots (Plate 44). The blocks themselves were joined with machine-stitching. The quilt top was backed, filled with cotton flannel, and quilted. A woven wool binding was used to finish the quilt, and ball fringe was used for bunny tails.

The machine-appliquéd block is an excellent beginner's approach to quilt making. Several sketches in Figure 26 suggest a few of the possibilities of this method of joining blocks. This way of working is especially suitable for any abstract pattern of geometric forms.

Plate 44. "Bunnies." Details of eyes, whiskers and tails give the animals some personality. When appliqué and embroidery are finished, the quilt top is sewn to a filler and a backing with quilting stitches, which show here outlining the blocks.

Figure 26. These three quilt designs are all based on simple geometric forms appliquéd to alternating blocks, which are joined in rows. Appliqué may be done by hand as well as by machine.

In working out a pattern based on repeated block designs, first cut an assortment of blocks and try them in different arrangements. When a satisfactory arrangement is arrived at, start cutting appliqué pieces—going back to change the original arrangement if necessary. These blocks could, of course, be hand-sewn instead of machine-sewn. Your problem is primarily one of working out an overall design.

Machine-appliquéd blocks, joined in a kind of ingenious jigsaw puzzle, combine certain characteristics of traditional quilts with a contemporary approach. In a detail of "Therese Quilt," Plate 45 shows the stitches that join the puzzle. The overall effect of this piecing is seen in Plate 46. The pattern of hexagonal shapes is so reminiscent of old quilts that it is a delightful jolt to have the faces emerge from the pattern.

Plate 47 shows a detail of "Bridget Quilt." Therese May, who designed and made these quilts, describes her approach this way: "The first step is to choose a photograph, preferably a slide, and project it onto a piece of paper, tracing with a pencil and selecting lines and shapes which simplify the picture and make it into a kind of jigsaw puzzle. This is then transferred to a ditto stencil or any other suitable means of reproduction in order to get 100 copies, or however many you need for your quilt.

"Then, putting these patterns aside, you cut 100 squares (or whatever shape you are using) of muslin, and 100 squares of assorted materials. Then you take the patterns and attach them to the assorted squares with staples and cut out all the little pieces of all 100 jigsaw puzzles, arranging them in little piles, and being careful not to lose any. I used muffin tins to keep them straight.

"Next you rearrange the pieces on the muslin squares, with each picture made up from various prints. Appliqué them with the zigzag. If no pieces are lost, you should end up with 100 little completed jigsaw puzzles. These, then, can be arranged with some other design element or by themselves.

"I didn't use a frame for my quilts; I just put the pieces together on the machine trying to keep them as flat as possible. Then I spread the quilt out on the floor, right side up, and put the lining material over that, face down. This was pinned all over to keep it in place. I machine-stitched all around the edges except for a little opening, turned it right side out, hand-stitched the opening, laid the quilt flat again, and put the knots in. I didn't use any middle layer as it was already heavy with muslin."

In "Therese Quilt," the knots are tied in the dark squares which separate the hexagonal portrait panels of the girl. Yarn is stitched through and tied on the quilt top. "Bridget Quilt" is shown in Color Plate 24, where the secondary pattern of diagonals and large forms appear more clearly.

Plate 45. "Therese Quilt" (detail) by Therese McMahan May. A hexagonal block is machine-appliquéd with jigsaw pieces of fabric forming a face in this contemporary merging of photo-image drawing with traditional quilt block.

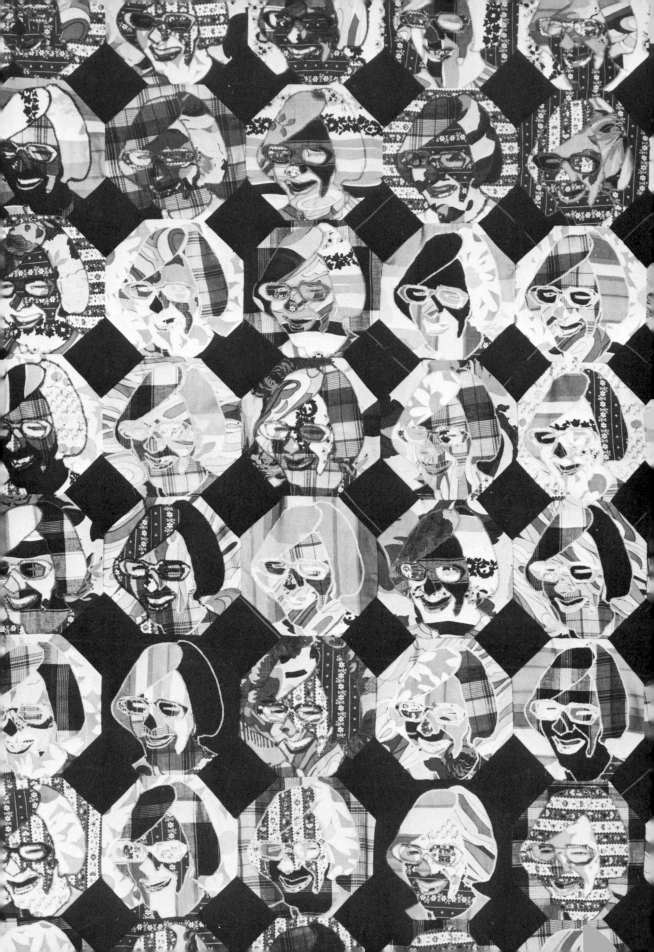

Plate 46. "Therese Quilt"; 72" by 90". The ingenious piecing of these blocks produces a quilt in which no two blocks are identical, and yet each repeats the others in design.

Plate 47. "Bridget Quilt" (detail) by Therese McMahan May. A photograph provides the basic block design in combining these varied textures and patterns.

2. Joining Plain, Printed & Dye-Designed Fabrics

The piecing together of numerous shapes cut from plain or printed fabrics forms one of the most basic means of quilt design. Traditionally quilts were often in geometric patterns repeated in either block or overall design. Phyllis Palmer and Ann Saunderson have made quilts which are contemporary versions of this, as seen in Color Plates 15 and 16. The crazy quilt or patchwork uses a similar though non-repeat arrangement. In either case, the design results from the mosaic-like arrangement of the many small pieces. Figure 27 shows one of the simplest patchworks. Striped fabrics used in such a crazy quilt produce an active overall pattern.

Figure 27. The basic patchwork or crazy-quilt approach, using striped fabrics, produces a very active pattern.

Contemporary versions of this mosaic approach are used by many quilt makers. One of the most unique quilts combining areas of small geometric repeats along with large open areas of solid color is Joan Lintault's "La Chola en La Colcha" (Plate 48). The background moves easily from the nostalgia of a precise, tight, traditional block repeat to the loose, less structured, contemporary pattern. Then, rising amidst all the blocks is the raised, padded figure of a girl. The quilt is thus "occupied" even when not in use.

Plate 48. "La Chola en La Colcha" by Joan Lintault; 86" by 104". Traditional, geometric piecing is combined with padded and quilted figure.

Plate 49. "La Chola en La Colcha" (detail).
The stitching and stuffing of the hand
causes it to rise from the surface of the
quilt.

Plate 50. "La Chola en La Colcha" (detail).
Small blocks show the detailed stitches
of piecing and quilting.

The result is both startling and humorous. Details of the hand and the piecing are shown in Plates 49 and 50. The blocks were all joined by hand with an overcast stitch, then quilted.

A very simple method of piecing is that used in "Yellow Bands" (Plate 51). Strips about 2 inches wide are cut in random lengths. These are then joined at the ends to provide long strips of material. Make each strip as long as the desired width of the finished quilt. These may be machine-sewn, though thread-ends should always be tied. Press seams open and then join the strips together horizontally. The completed pieced top can then be lined, padded and quilted. Plate 51 shows the quilting which outlines each of the small pieces. This method of piecing could be adapted to bands of any size. Very narrow ones would be more complex and more heavily stitched; wide ones, almost brick sized, could be quickly assembled. Plate 52 shows the reverse side of "Yellow Bands" and the quilting pattern which occurs on the back.

Plate 51. "Yellow Bands" (detail) by the author. Rectangles of gold and yellow cottons are joined into bands to form this pieced quilt.

Plate 52. "Yellow Bands" (reverse side). Quilting stitches, following the bands, carry the pattern through to the back of the quilt.

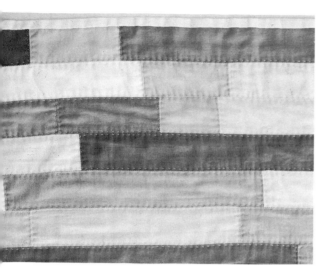

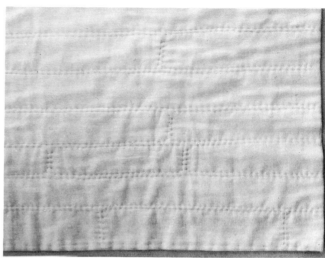

Piecing for the quilt in Plate 53 shows a patchwork approach in deep red and yellow. Pieces are all machine-sewn with no regard for "straight" of fabric or bias cut. The overall pattern of dark and light is active and energetic, resulting in part from an "unplanned" effect where the darks of one section join a dark area in another and new shapes emerge. The quilt was photographed after being pieced, though no quilting had been done.

Plate 53. "CHLBDCOG-8" (detail) by Brother Martin Verducci, O.P. Bright red and yellow fabrics cut in haphazard blocks of various sizes form new shapes when the blocks are joined.

Another approach to the pieced top is to predesign the fabric. Maureen Nichelson's "Large Batik Quilt" (Plate 57) uses blocks cut mainly from batiked fabrics. Even most of the striped fabrics were produced by batik, which gives a variation and richness to the stripes. The scale of the fabric patterns was planned in terms of the block size as well as for its effect in the overall quilt. The result is a dynamic design, one which continues to intrigue the viewer, right down to the tiniest lined details (Plate 58) of the wax-and-dye process. Unfortunately, batik is too complex a process to cover adequately in this book. If you are already familiar with the process, you can experiment with its use for quilt making. If batik is new to you, consult one of the many excellent reference books available for detailed information on the process.

Plate 58. "Large Batik Quilt" (detail). The bold design and the fine-line details were both achieved by carefully controlled use of the batik process.

Tie-dye offers another means of designing fabrics. Molly Sue Hanner has made particularly good use of it in her pieced quilt top (Plates 59 and 60). Panels of material were tie-dyed first. Then these panels were cut into sections of various sizes and joined together in new arrangements.

Tie-dye, in its simplest form, is easy to do, though many complex variations are possible. Essentially the process is one of binding the fabric so it will resist color in the tied areas. Fabric is gathered and tied tightly with waxed string, wire or cord. Then the material is dipped in a dye bath. When the tying is tight, the dye cannot penetrate, thus leaving areas of pattern in the original fabric color. A series of different-colored dye baths allows colors to mix and develop rich variations. The tying itself is very important; gathering or folding the material across the width of the fabric will form a design in a horizontal pattern. Drawing up a bit of fabric, like the tip of an unopened umbrella, before tie-dyeing it will produce a circular or medallion-like design.

Molly Sue Hanner has combined various kinds of tie-dye in her quilt, and she exhibits a great control over the dye method. She exerts equal control in the overall pattern, which incorporates horizontal designs, small medallions and circles. The medallions have been cut and reassembled, so that the pattern continues over a varying background. The plain, solid blocks in both dark and light colors are a necessary foil for her complex patterns.

Plate 59. "Tie-Dye Quilt" by Molly Sue Hanner. Piecing produces an overall pattern of diagonal, vertical, and horizontal lines that purposefully contrast with the tie-dyed, circular medallion forms.

Plate 60. "Tie-Dye Quilt" (detail). Dye-designed fabrics are cut and reassembled to re-form the medallion patterns with a background of changing color.

Dyeing designs into the material or printing them on can be achieved by any technique that permanently affects the colors. Besides batik and tie-dye, silk-screening is among the most common and versatile methods. Photo silk-screen methods would make it possible to reproduce faces, scenes, groups, buildings, etc., with stitching and padding used to embellish and emphasize these shapes. Plates 22 and 30 showed a limited use of screening, but it is an area of great potential.

Permanent textile paints or permanent inks may be used in designing without stencils. Some laundry markers and marking pens are colorfast, and these are also suitable. The only materials to avoid are those which stiffen the fabric and make it difficult to sew through. Latex paints are certainly permanent and do not come out in the laundry if they are allowed to dry before being washed. Though they are not recommended as fabric paints, they can be used if you avoid putting a heavy application of paint on those areas where you intend to sew. This can be partly controlled by your cutting. Many of the permanent inks and paints make direct application of fine details possible, thus enabling you to use quotations, dates, names, poetry, songs or personal commentary as part of your quilt design.

3. Joining Prestuffed Units

There are several ways of prestuffing the blocks or sections of the pieced quilt which make the final assembly a simple matter. One of the easiest of these methods is shown in Plate 61. A piece of fabric is cut (here taffetas and silk linings were used), folded over, and sewn together along two edges (Figure 28). This sewn piece is then turned right side out, and it is stuffed with cotton or Dacron batting. Use sheet-form batting, and cut sections to slide into the "pocket" of material. Cut two to four layers, depending upon how "fat" you want the individual pillow to be.

Figure 28. A piece of fabric is folded over and sewn together on two sides, then turned right side out. Stuffing is inserted and the open seam is slip-stitched closed.

After making a number of these stuffed forms, start fitting them together. Slip-stitch the open end closed after you determine it is the right size. You can adjust the size of a block by turning a little more or less of the material under for the last hem. Then slip-stitch the blocks together (Figure 29). Two rows of stitching, one done from the front and one from the reverse side, will give you a firm connection. Some blocks may have to be cut to fit specific spots. You can simplify assembly by cutting according to a modular unit plan, such as 4 inches by 4 inches, 4 by 8 inches, etc. The blocks can then be tied in the center to hold the batting in place. (See Color Plate 17.)

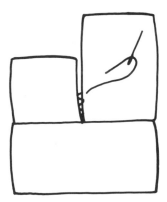

Figure 29. Finished pillow forms are joined by hand-sewing.

Plate 61. "Pillow Quilt" (detail) by the author. Small pillow forms, sewn and stuffed, are then joined so that the quilt is finished as you go.

Appliqué blocks can also be sewn and stuffed before being pieced to each other (Figure 30). Two rectangles of fabric are cut to the same size. (This same size is then used for all the blocks.) One rectangle is appliquéd with a design. The second piece of fabric is placed over the first so that the edges can be sewn on three sides. The sewn form is then turned, and a piece of cotton batting cut to fit inside is slipped into place. The remaining edge is stitched shut. Then a quilting stitch is used to outline the blocks and the appliqué (Plate 62). When a number of blocks are completed, they may be joined by slip-stitching at both front and back.

 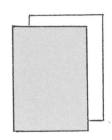 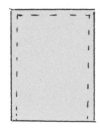 

Figure 30. A rectangle is appliquéd and placed face down over another piece of fabric of the same size. The two pieces are sewn together on three sides; the block is turned right side out again and stuffed before the open edge is stitched shut. Such appliquéd blocks are joined in the same manner as the pillow blocks.

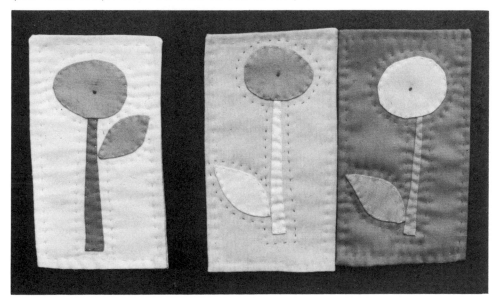

Plate 62. "Flowers" (detail) by the author. Each appliquéd block has its own backing and filler and is quilted individually. When you have a series of blocks, you can join them with slip stitches.

Plate 63 shows a block made with "cut-through" appliqué. In this technique, four or five pieces of fabric, in varying colors, are cut to the same size and stacked together. This gives the quilt block its thickness. After the stack is basted at the outside edges, the design is achieved by cutting through the layers of fabric to the colors underneath. Each raw edge is turned under and appliquéd to the fabric beneath with a blind stitch. However, the thickness of all the fabrics combined at the outside edges of the stack makes it difficult to finish those edges by hemming or turning them under. These blocks are therefore joined with strips of fabric instead of with slip-stitching.

Plate 64 shows prefinished cut-through blocks after they have been joined with bands of fabric. The bands on the front were added by machine-stitching. On the reverse side (seen in Plate 65), one edge of each band was machine-stitched at the same time as the corresponding edge in front, but the last edge had to be sewn down by hand.

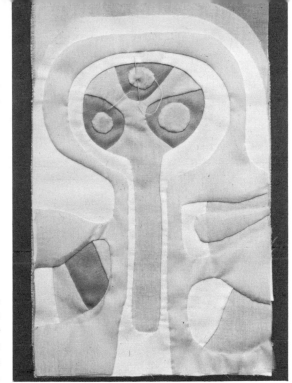

Plate 63. "Cut-Through Quilt Block" by the author. Raised or puffy edges result from the blind stitch that attaches each cut edge to the fabric beneath it. Four or five layers are stacked and the design appears as you cut one layer to reveal another.

Plate 64. "Cut-Through Quilt" (detail) by the author. A cut-through block has raw edges that are too thick to be turned under and hemmed. Strips of fabric are added to both the front and back of the blocks to finish them and to join them to each other.

Plate 65. "Cut-Through Quilt" (detail, reverse side). For a finished look, one edge of each strip on the back must be turned under and sewn by hand.

To do a cut-through quilt, all of the cut-through blocks should be the same height. Bands can then be added at the two vertical sides, as shown in Figure 31. When a number of blocks have been joined, you will have a horizontal row. Another band of material is used horizontally between the rows to connect them. The blocks could also be bound individually and then slip-stitched together (Figure 32). The cut-through appliqué is more difficult than regular appliqué and would not be the best means for a first effort at quilt making. Prestuffed blocks of some other kind would be preferable.

For either the beginner or the advanced quilt maker, the prestuffed blocks have certain advantages. They provide a decorative, padded bed cover, though a quilting frame is never required. The work is finished as you go along. It provides a means of working which is simple to handle but unlimited in variations. Your own ideas for variations will occur to you as you sew. If you enjoy quilt making, there is a whole world of new ideas and new experiences awaiting you.

Figure 31. Blocks of cut-through appliqué are joined with fabric strips of a contrasting color to make a horizontal row of blocks. Rows are then joined to one another by the addition of a horizontal band of fabric. Drawing shows addition of bands on the front only.

Figure 32. Another means of finishing the cut-through block is to edge each one with a binding and then slip-stitch the blocks together.

Part III

QUILTING

Quilting is the means by which we attach a quilt top to its backing fabric and a filler. Putting a quilt together is a sandwiching process. The outside layers provide top and bottom, and a filler is used between. The quilting stitch goes through all three layers, binding them firmly together. However, the stitching is not merely functional; it is also an important visual part of the total design.

Accomplished through the use of a small running stitch, the quilting may serve to embellish the blocks, to outline the pieces, or to give emphasis to the appliqué of the quilt top. Or the quilting may become the prime decorative element on a plain or solid color top. Your needle becomes a drawing tool, leaving behind it a trailing line of thread. Quilting offers that marvelous opportunity to combine the practical and aesthetic, for here stitches serve both as the binding element and as linear drawings.

Part III describes quilting with a frame as well as quilting without a frame. Directions are given for the quilting process from the selection of materials to the binding of the finished quilt.

Plate 66. "A Midwinter Day-Mare" by Else Brown; 66" by 90". Machine embroidery on the fabric top produces both the design and the quilting pattern; combined with the padding, the stitching throws the design into relief and creates a sculptured surface.

1. The Quilting Process

In making quilts, most of us expend our excitement and energies on the quilt top, where our selections of colors, contrasts, patterns and shapes are apparent. We have the large, overall pattern or design and the smaller collection of shapes which produces it. We also often have an intermediate unit of the individual blocks. But, of equal importance, we have the quilting stitches themselves. It is in these stitches that we are given a final opportunity to diversify scale.

Perhaps one of the most intriguing elements in quilts is the way in which certain aspects grow or diminish in importance depending upon your relationship to them. As work on the quilt progresses, you tend to lose sight of the overall design because new elements of pattern appear. The knowledge that there is always more to be seen within the overall design seems aesthetically vital to the enjoyment of the total quilt. Other elements, another pattern on a smaller scale, lead you to new details. You are always on the brink of new discoveries.

This, then, is one of the primary values of the quilting stitch. It offers a final small-scale pattern through the length of the stitches, the color of the thread, the finely gathered lines of fabric around the stitches, and the little variations that occur within the framework of one quilter's "style." Quilting adds another dimension. It has been explored for its own sake in many early American quilts, in which the quilting stitch alone provides the total quilt design. The stitches become a web of richly varied lines as in a drawing.

Else Brown's imaginative and surrealistic "A Midwinter Day-Mare" (Plate 66) shows the way in which the sewing machine was used as though it were a drawing pencil. A detail of the quilt (Plate 67) shows the delicacy of the machine stitch as a single line and the variation in the weight of each line, depending upon the number of times the particular line was repeated.

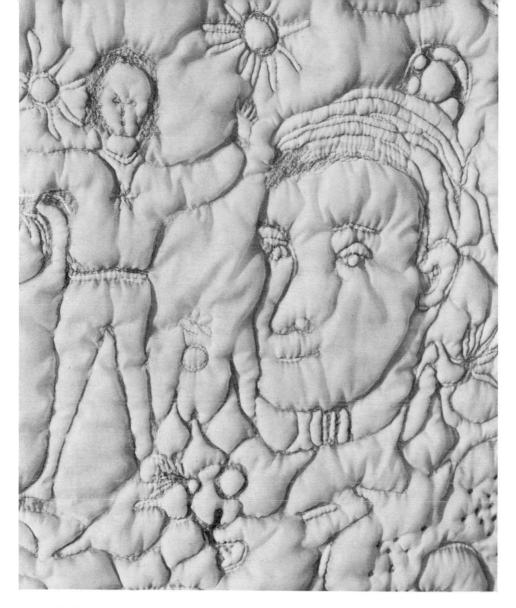

Plate 67. "A Midwinter Day-Mare" (detail). The sewing machine draws, with lines of thread, an outline of figures and forms. Stitches vary from a light, single line to heavy collections of many lines.

Because it is difficult to handle three large layers of material with a sewing machine, this quilt was stuffed *after* the design was stitched. The method, called trapunto, gives the same sculptural effect to the surface as does hand-stitching the design through the three layers. An example of the latter technique was seen in Plate 3, page 24. "A Midwinter Day-Mare" was begun with a full-sized piece of fabric for the top. This was a single 90-inch length of Dacron 66 inches wide.

Next, a piece of nylon net was cut to the same size as the quilt top. The net comes in a 72-inch width, so it was not necessary to piece it. The nylon net was basted to the wrong side of the top piece with a grid of stitches that held the two pieces firmly together, as shown in Figure 33.

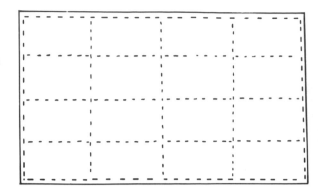

Figure 33. Intersecting lines of basting stitches attach nylon net to the wrong side of the Dacron top in preparation for trapunto stitching.

With the aid of a darning foot on the sewing machine, the design was freely stitched on the right side of the base material. This "freewheeling" stitch, with the machine's feed-dogs lowered and the presser foot raised, made it possible to guide the stitching easily over the surface.

After being stitched, the quilt top was turned wrong side up and the nylon net was slit in the center of each area that was to be padded. The areas were stuffed with Dacron batting; then each slitted opening was sewn closed with a line of slip stitches. A thin, wooden rod was used to help push the Dacron stuffing into small areas between the lines of stitching.

A lining was cut the same size as the quilt top and basted to the right side of the top, with the finished surfaces face to face. The lining and top were machine-sewn at three of the outer edges and then the sewn pieces were turned right side out, producing a form like a huge pillowcase. The opening at the end was stitched closed with a slip stitch.

The finished quilt design is a combination of imagery and rounded forms that invite you to run your hands over the surface. The images themselves are both commonplace and mysterious—birds, faces, figures, trees, flowers and hands become enmeshed, merging into and growing out of one another. Together, the stitching and the padding create a unified design. Whether all three layers of the quilt are stitched at one time or the padding is inserted later, the principle remains the same.

Even when quilting is used basically as a utilitarian device, it assumes an importance in the overall scale of the quilt. The workmanship adds an essential quality which is not determined by design. Quilting should therefore be viewed with an eye to its potential in the total success and effect of the quilt.

The use of quilting stitches as an integral part of the quilt top is essential for a completely satisfying design. The quilting stitch must not be something which imposes its pattern over another pattern. The two must emerge together, and the relationship between them enhances both and produces a new total effect.

A beautiful example of this relationship is seen in Plate 68, a quilt by Charles Counts and the Rising Fawn Quilters. A simple form is appliquéd to the white quilt top. This basic shape produces the central theme around which the quilting is developed. It grows in lines and spirals, echoing the same tree form and giving emphasis to the appliquéd form. Plate 69 shows another example of the beautifully integrated patterns of appliqué and quilting.

Plate 68. "Quilt" by Charles Counts and the Rising Fawn Quilters. The lines of the quilting echo the forms suggested by the appliqué on the quilt top.

Plate 69. "Quilt" by Charles Counts and the Rising Fawn Quilters. Beautifully integrated patterns of quilting and appliqué illustrate the potential of relating these two forms.

Occasionally the layers of the quilt are held together without stitching, by tacking the pieces with yarn tied or knotted at intervals over the quilt top. The tied ends of the yarn may appear on the top or on the reverse side of the quilt, and they may be cut as short as ½ of an inch or they may extend as long as a couple of inches, depending upon the importance the quilt maker wishes to give to the knotting pattern.

Plate 70 shows an example of this knotting and tying. Here a flannel filler and a cotton backing were used under a pale yellow top. Yarn was stitched down through all three layers, then back up so that the two ends emerged on the top side of the quilt, where they were tied together. Yarns of different weights can be tied so that the knots produce patterns of spacing on the top. Plate 71 shows the reverse side of the quilt. On a solid-color fabric, as was used here, it is helpful to place a penciled dot to keep the knots in a specific order or placement. The knots can also be used in a random pattern.

The tying may be done with bright-colored yarns or with any other material (string, cord, etc.) that can be drawn through the fabric and which will hold a knot. When the quilt is fully filled or padded, the ties give a puffy appearance, as characterized in what is sometimes called a "comforter." But the comforter is usually a plain, solid fabric, neither appliquéd nor pieced. The tying produces the only design element. Tying can also be used in a purely functional way to hold a coverlet to a lining or backing material. However, if the quilt top has been designed, then the plump filling and tying do little to enhance it, and the knotted threads should be made inconspicuous. The quilting stitch, on the other hand, can be used to define the piecing or the appliqué design, setting it off and emphasizing each shape and form.

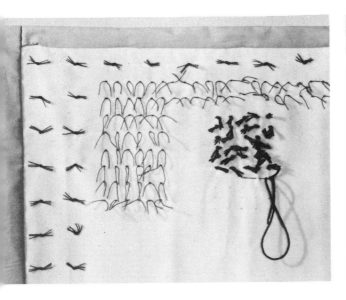

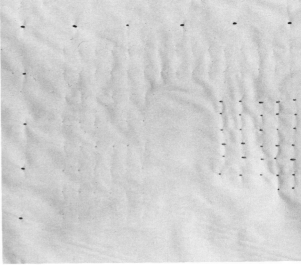

Plate 70. Tied Comforter (detail) by the author. Yarns tie the backing, filler and velvet top together with a pattern of knots.

Plate 71. Tied Comforter (detail, reverse side). Backs of the knots form a pattern of dots and puckers on the underside of the quilt.

Plate 72. *"Grandma's Garden" by the author; 42" by 44". Laces, edgings, and doilies are collected in this delicate white-on-white quilt. Quilting stitches outline and repeat the appliquéd forms.*

Plate 73. "Grandma's Garden" (detail). Stems are created from edgings of lace; leaves are formed with net, organza and bits of embroidery. These pieces are appliquéd with a machine-sewn satin stitch.

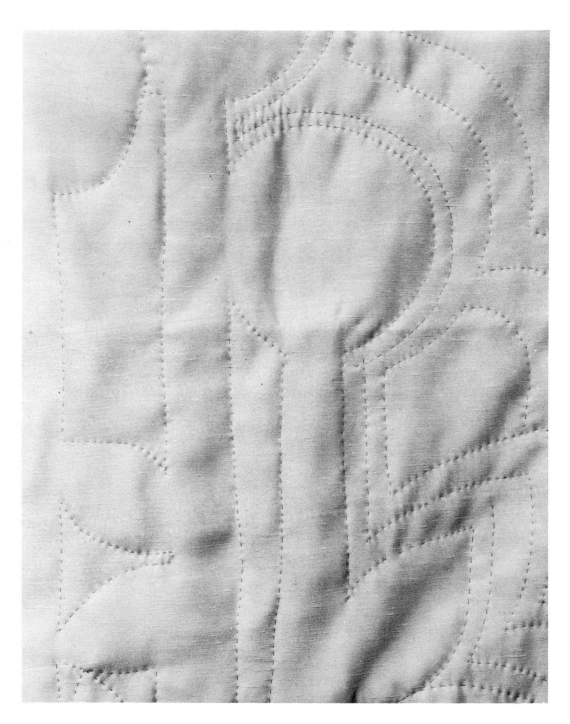

Plate 74. "Grandma's Garden" (reverse side, detail). Quilting stitches show the forms of leaves and flowers on the back.

The quilting stitches in "Grandma's Garden" (Plate 72) outline and repeat the shapes of the delicate floral pattern appliqué. Transparent and semi-transparent fabrics, such as organdy, net, and organza were machine-stitched to the quilt top to form stems and leaves. The blossoms were fashioned from handmade lace doilies. The old doilies and antimacassars, which seem so out of place in contemporary homes, are complex and intricate linear drawings that can be incorporated into a contemporary design. Plate 73 shows a detail of the appliqué and the quilting stitches. The stitching goes through the cotton flannel filler and appears as a pattern on the reverse side of the quilt (Plate 74).

The quilting process may be new to many beginning quilt makers. But it is a simple process, and one that is easily mastered. However, if quilt tops are your primary interest, it is sometimes possible to find quilters who will take your quilt top through the final stages. Many church groups still do this as a means of fund raising. Charges are usually made by the spool; that way you pay more for more intricate quilting and less for very simple quilting. If you find an individual or a group to quilt for you, be sure you have a clear understanding of the quilting pattern before work is begun. Even if you do not execute the quilting yourself, you should be familiar with the process involved.

The best way to learn quilting is to select a small, beginning project—a crib quilt, or a fabric to be quilted for a pillow or skirt. Any of these small projects can be quilted without the use of a frame on which to stretch the layers flat.

Quilts up to about 3 feet by 5 feet seem to me to be more easily quilted without a frame. Some women never use a frame, regardless of the size of a quilt. Others use either a frame or a quilting hoop for all quilting, no matter how large or small. The quilting hoop is similar to an embroidery hoop, though much larger, and it is usually attached to a base so that the angle and height of the working surface can be adjusted. A quilting frame is an adjustable, four-sided device to which the quilt layers are attached. Whether or not you use a frame in quilting will be a matter of your own preference after having experimented with and without it.

Once a quilt top is completed, the filler or padding must be selected. Several different materials are available; the final choice depends upon how you intend to quilt and the desired appearance of the finished piece. Cotton batting is probably the most common filler. It is inexpensive and readily available. When it is unrolled, it provides a large, flat, uniformly thick piece of batting the size of an average quilt. This cotton batting must be quilted fairly closely, as the stitches are needed to hold the batting in place. If rows of quilting stitches are too far apart, the batting will shift when the quilt is washed, and will become "lumpy."

A second material suitable for filler is Dacron or other synthetic batting. It is more expensive than cotton, but very resilient and easy to sew through. It does not "lump" as readily as the cotton; however, it also is best suited where stitching lines of the quilting are fairly close. Any spaces larger than 3 or 4 inches square would allow the batting to slip during washing or through continued use. The advantage of using batting is its thickness or bulk. The thickness of the batting material makes the quilted design stand out in strong relief.

Cotton "sheet" blankets provide excellent filler for quilts. The blankets must be washed and shrunk before being used, but the primary advantage is that there will be no shifting or lumping when the quilt is washed. No matter how little quilting occurs in some areas, the filler remains in place. This cotton flannel makes a soft, durable filler that is easy to handle. Regular cotton flannel purchased by the yard is also suitable, though it would need to be pieced to make a panel large enough for most quilts.

Rather than piece cotton flannel by making machine-sewn lines, just let one piece of flannel slightly overlap the next, then baste the two pieces together. One result of using cotton flannel as filler is that the finished quilt is flatter than one using batting. For an appliqué top this may be an advantage, as it allows the appliqué design to remain prominent. Where the quilting design is to be prominent, thicker filler is best.

Other possibilities for filler are muslin and any nonshrinking, synthetic blanket. The selection is made in terms of the desired weight of the finished quilt, as well as desired thickness. The main advantage of using either a fabric or a blanket instead of batting is that the necessity of close quilting is eliminated. Since the quilting should relate to the design of the quilt top, close quilting is not always desirable. On some appliquéd blocks, the quilting might be quite limited, outlining the block and its appliquéd forms. On quilts in which the quilting stitches are a dominant or equal part of the design, batting can easily be held in place.

With your quilt top prepared and the filler selected, you now need a fabric for the quilt backing. This may be a solid color or a print; it should be lightweight enough to sew through easily, and should relate in some way to the front of the quilt. It can be similar in color, it can repeat an accent color, or it can be a print that has been used in the appliqué. When this fabric is prepared to size, you are ready to place the layers for quilting.

To quilt without a frame, the large piece of fabric for the quilt backing is placed on a table top or floor with any seams pressed open and facing up. Place filler on the backing and the quilt top, face up, on top of that. Both filler and backing should extend beyond the edges of the quilt top. If they do not, additional material should be added to each until several spare inches are allowed. See Figure 34 for this placement.

Figure 34. The quilt is basically a three-layered sandwich of backing material, filler, and decorative top. Both filler and backing should extend beyond the edges of the top.

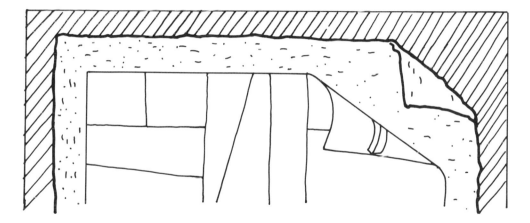

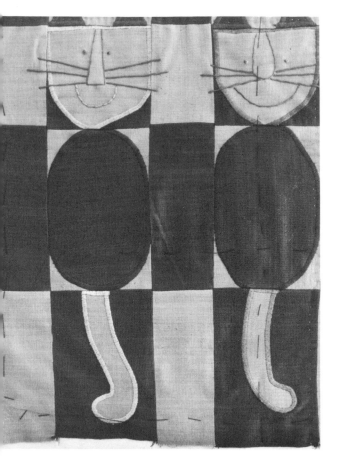

above, left:
Plate 75. "Cats" (detail) by the author. After blocks are joined, the top is basted to a flannel filler and a backing.

above, right:
Plate 76. "Cats" (detail). When the layers are quilted, the stitches are placed inside each block.

left:
Plate 77. "Cats" (reverse side, detail). Quilting stitches repeat pattern of both the blocks and the appliqué on the back of the quilt.

When all three layers are spread and smoothed flat, they should be pinned together and then basted. Basting stitches need not be tiny or time-consuming. Make them large. Two diagonal rows, one horizontal and one vertical row of stitching in addition to a row around the perimeter of the quilt top would be adequate. See Figure 35 for a suggestion on basting stitches. Check the back side of the quilt to be sure that there are no folds or gathers in the material. If any occur, remove that row of basting and re-do it, starting from the center and smoothing the materials out towards the edges.

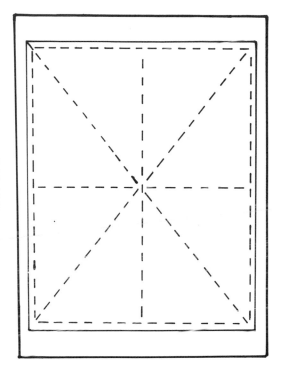

Figure 35. When the layers have been stacked and smoothed, they are pinned and basted together. Several intersecting lines of basting will keep the layers in place.

The needle you select for quilting is primarily a matter of what is most comfortable for you to use. For my own work, a short, sharp quilting needle (a number eight or nine) seems best. Longer needles often bend, but some quilters don't feel "at home" with a needle until it *is* slightly bent. Each person you talk with, and each reference you consult, will offer a differing opinion on how the quilting is accomplished, what needle to use, and how many stitches to take at one time. As you work, you will develop your own preferences and methods. What is most important to remember is that any needle and any approach will work, so long as it works for *you*.

Concerning the manner of working, some quilters insist that quilting must start from the center and work out to the sides. Others recommend starting at one side and working across to the other side. Still others find they can work from both sides, ending up in the center. The first approach, working from the center out, seems to me to be best, since it allows for any unevenness or fullness to be worked out to the edges. It may not be the method that works best for you. The length of the needle, how you take your stitches, the fineness of the quilting—all blend into a rhythm of sewing.

Quilting stitches should be kept small. The number of stitches taken at one time depends in part upon the fullness of the filler, the weight of the fabrics, and how tightly the quilt might be stretched if it is on a frame. Some quilters take several stitches at once; others insist that the best results are achieved only when stitches are taken one at a time. Two or three stitches at a time seem to be easily handled, especially if the filler is lightweight.

Quilting thread is usually available, though not always in a complete color range. These threads are strong and smooth, making it easy to draw the thread through the material. They do not twist or knot easily as you sew. If quilting thread is not available, you can use a chunk of dressmaker's beeswax on a #50 or #60 thread. Just drawing the threaded needle through the wax will coat it adequately; then wipe off any excess wax that is visible. You may quilt with plain, unwaxed thread. Whether your thread color matches or contrasts with the fabric color depends upon the kind of emphasis you wish to give to the quilting stitches. It often helps to quilt a small, sample piece in various colors to aid in this decision. Generally, a color which blends without matching exactly or contrasting strongly is best.

The quilting stitches can start at the center and work out towards the top, bottom and sides. Or they may all go all the way across in one direction, then all the way across at right angles. You will find which way is easiest for you. Figure 36 suggests possible directions for quilting stitches. It is generally easier, if you are right-handed, to sew from right to left, and from left to right if you are left-handed. It is always easier to sew towards yourself rather than away from yourself.

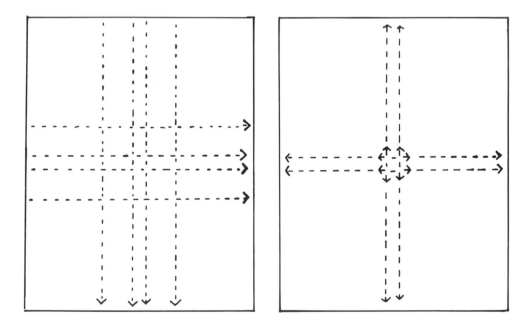

Figure 36. Quilting stitches can start at one edge of the top and move all the way across, or they can start at the center and work out to the edges.

Quilting is a simple in-and-out stitch. In quilting without a frame, you can easily place one hand under the quilt, keeping your sewing hand on top. Because the material is not stretched over a frame, the stitching is easy to accomplish. Keep the quilt flat on a table top as you sew. That way, you will avoid most problems in keeping the quilt from puckering or becoming uneven. Continue quilting until you have reached all the edges and you will then be ready to bind or finish the quilt. Binding is described later in this chapter.

Quilting with a frame will greatly simplify the joining of a large-sized quilt. A frame can be assembled for use, then taken apart for storage. The frame offers a means of holding the layers together and even, and of keeping them slightly taut for quilting.

The easiest way to make a frame is to use four lengths of wood cut from standard lumber stock measuring either 2 inches wide by 2 inches thick or 2 inches wide by 1 inch thick. Hardwood is sturdy and can be sanded smooth, but pine also serves the purpose well. Two of the wood strips should be 6 inches longer than the width of the quilt, which will be attached to these rails. The other two strips, which will act as stretchers between the rails, need not be longer than 3 feet. This is because it is not easy to reach in more than about 2 feet from each side rail in order to sew; therefore, only a portion of the quilt's length is exposed at one time, the rest being rolled up on the rails.

The stretchers are added to support the rails (Figure 37). C-clamps may be used to secure the stretchers and rails at the corners. Another convenient means is to drill a hole in the end of each rail and a series of holes in the stretchers. Then a peg or a bolt slipped into place, with a nut or key to hold it, will keep the corners of the frame firmly in place (Figures 38 and 39).

Figure 37. To do the quilting on a very large top, the quilt may have to be placed crosswise on a frame of rails and stretchers, with the length rolled up on the rails.

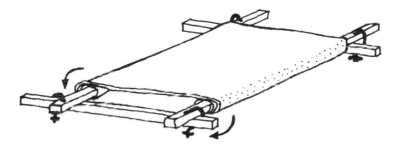

Figure 38. The rails and stretchers are attached at the corners to keep the frame steady. A system of holes and pegs makes the frame adjustable.

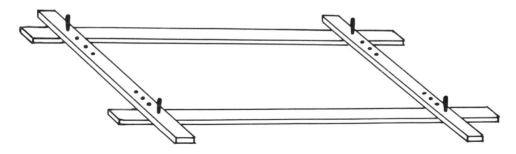

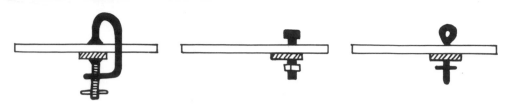

Figure 39. The corners of the frame may also be fastened with C-clamps, with a nut and bolt, or with a pin and key.

In order to attach the quilt to the frame, the rails must have fabric added to them. This can be done by tacking or stapling a length of twill tape to each rail so that one edge of the tape projects out from the rail (Figure 40a). Another method is to cover the rail with muslin or ticking, stapling the material so that there is a short flap of fabric extending from the rail (Plate 78 and Figure 40b). The quilt backing is then pinned and sewn to the tape or fabric (Figure 40c).

Prepare the quilt backing by spreading it out flat on a large table or on the floor. Place it right side down, so that if it has been pieced the seams will face up and will be on the inside of the quilt. The backing must be several inches larger in each dimension than the quilt top. The rails are then placed at the ends of the quilt (along the width) and the backing material is sewn to the tape or muslin of the rail with small basting stitches. More than one row of basting stitches may be required to hold the backing firmly.

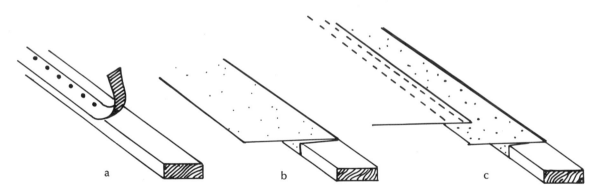

Figure 40. Fabric must be attached to the rails to hold the quilt. This is done by tacking a strip of twill tape in place (a), or muslin can be stapled or tacked and wrapped once around the rail (b). The backing material of the quilt is then attached to the muslin or twill tape with a large running stitch (c).

Plate 78. Each rail of the quilting frame has fabric stapled in place. A C-clamp joins the rails to a stretcher at each corner.

Once the backing is basted to the rails, the material is smoothed flat and the batting or filler is placed on top. The filler is also cut larger than the quilt top. Plate 79 shows the backing basted to the rail and the filler laid on the backing.

Next the quilt top is placed, face up, over the filler (Plate 80). These two layers and the backing are all tacked together with basting stitches that start at the center and go out towards corners, top, and bottom, as was shown in Figure 35. Care must be taken to see that all layers are kept smooth and free of wrinkles or folds.

When basting is completed, the quilt is rolled up on the rails until only about 3 feet of the quilt top remains exposed. (Each rail is rolled towards the center of the quilt. The rail on the left side is rolled counterclockwise; the one on the right, clockwise.) Then the stretchers are attached. The C-clamps or pegs are put in place to hold the quilt somewhat taut, though not so tight that there is any stretching of the material or stitches. At this point the end of the quilt should look like Figure 41.

The exposed ends towards the stretchers must now be held in place. This may be done either with a series of long and heavy stitches binding the fabric to the frame (Figure 42), or it may be done with pieces of tape pinned in place (Figure 43 and Plate 81).

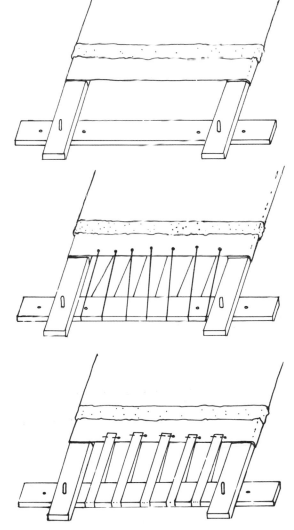

Figure 41. The quilt is rolled onto the rails until only part of the top is exposed. Then the stretchers are added and clamped or pegged into place.

Figure 42. The quilt is held in place on the stretchers by heavy thread or string wrapped around the wood and stitched to the backing's edge.

Figure 43. Tape strips drawn around the stretchers and pinned to the backing material is another way of holding the exposed part of the quilt taut on the stretchers.

Plate 79. Basting stitches hold the quilt backing to each rail. Dacron batting has been placed on top of the backing.

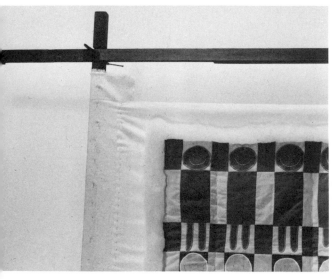

Plate 80. The quilt top is placed over the batting and the backing fabric, and the three layers are basted together.

Plate 81. Corners are loosened so that the quilt can be rolled onto the rails. When only about 2 or 3 feet of the quilt remains exposed, C-clamps are put into place. Quilt is then attached to stretchers by pinning tape to the backing material.

The next important step is to find a support to keep the frame at a height that is comfortable for quilting. A work surface that is too low will finish your spine long before you finish your quilt. For support, the frame can be rested on the arms of chairs or on the backs of low chairs. Sawhorses can also be used to support the frame. Some of the more elaborate frames have legs or supports built in as part of the frame. These are, of course, more difficult to store. The simple frame just described can be leaned up against a wall, out of the way, when work on the quilt is not in progress.

Quilting can begin when the frame has been clamped and supported. As soon as the exposed area of the quilt is finished, the corners of the frame are loosened and the rails are both moved either to the left or to the right until an unquilted area is exposed. This is quilted and a new area is exposed. Continue until one rail has been entirely unrolled and half the quilt has been stitched. Then reroll the quilt onto the empty rail until you reach the center, and finish the quilting in the opposite direction.

There are many other kinds of quilting frames, some with winding wheels and ratchets to simplify the rolling. The one described in this chapter can be made without extensive tools. In fact, you can purchase the wood precut, and using C-clamps allows you to handle the frame by yourself. This frame, while very simple, is adequate and is the only kind I have ever used. Should you pursue the building of a more elaborate frame, the most important details to watch for are comfort in seating, simple dismantling, and easy storage. A frame supported by chairs is the most practical one for most homes.

When the quilting is finished, the quilt must then be bound at the edges. This can be done in any of several ways. The quilt is first removed from the frame, and any basting stitches left in it must be removed. Figure 44 shows the preparation of a quilted top for binding. The filler was trimmed (after quilting) so that it extended 2 inches beyond the quilt top. The fabric of the backing material was trimmed to a 4½-inch extension. The amount of this extension determines the width of the finished border or binding. The extra backing fabric must be twice the width of the extending filler if the filler is to be covered. Then an additional ½ of an inch allows for a hem. See Figure 45, which shows the way the backing was then folded over the filler with the corners mitered. This gives a finished edge on both front and back.

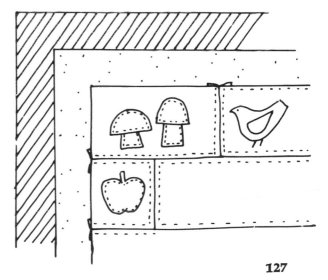

Figure 44. When quilting is completed, the quilt is removed from the frame and the edges are trimmed perfectly square, leaving enough extra filler and extra backing material for binding.

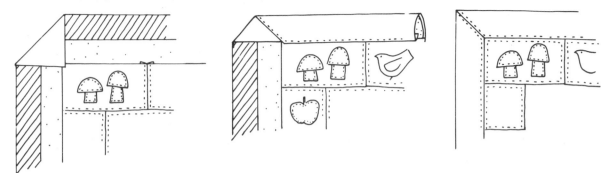

Figure 45. The extension of the quilt backing is folded over the filler so that all the edges are covered and each corner is mitered. The fabric is sewn down with a running stitch to bind the quilt.

Any prefinished binding may be used. Blanket binding, which is 2 inches wide, is easily sewn to the edge with a quilting stitch. Woven bindings and bias edgings are available in a good range of colors. Or fabric may be cut from materials used in the quilt and made into a self-binding. Figure 46 shows the steps in attaching strips of fabric for binding the edges.

After the quilt is finished, the enjoyment of using it is still in store. No quilt should be made only to be put away and saved for someone else's use "someday." A quilt's beauty can best be appreciated when it is *in* use. The time, energy, care and patience you have expended in sewing a quilt do not flourish in a bureau drawer. The finished quilt is durable, usable, washable (or cleanable) and it has not fulfilled its purpose until it is also used and enjoyed. Only then does the work offer a deep and lasting sense of accomplishment.

Figure 46. Separate strips of fabric may be used to bind the quilt. Sew each strip onto the quilt's front. Slip-stitch the other edge of each strip to the rear of the quilt.

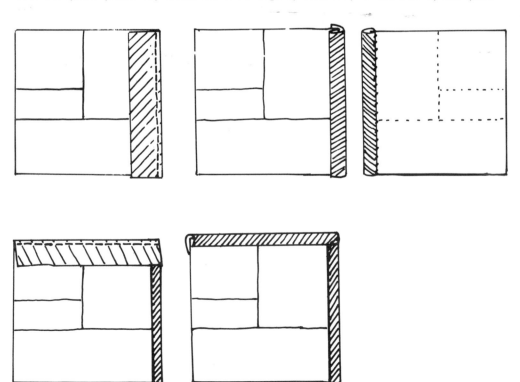